Praying with St Teresa

through

The Way of Perfection

JEROME LANTRY OCD

With a Foreword by James McCaffrey OCD

First published 2015 by:

TERESIAN PRESS
Carmelite Priory
Boars Hill
Oxford OX1 5HB
priory@carmelite.org.uk

ISBN 978-0-947916-16-9

A catalogue record for this book is available
from the British Library.

Cover image shows an icon by Sister Mary Grace,
copies of which are available from:
Carmelite Monastery, 59 Allendale, Terre Haute, IN 47802, USA
812-299-1410
www.heartsawake.org

Cover design by Joshua Horgan, Oxford

Typeset and printed by Joshua Horgan, Oxford

Contents

Foreword

In this year, 2015, when the Church throughout the world is celebrating the five hundredth anniversary of the birth of St Teresa of Avila, it is a pleasure to bring out a new edition of *Praying with St Teresa*, a small gem by Fr Jerome Lantry, OCD. The earlier version of this book, entitled *Saint Teresa on Prayer*, was brought out by the Discalced Carmelite friars of England and Ireland in 1981 and has always been extremely well received. This new edition, in which the work has undergone a small number of revisions and additions, has been brought out not only to mark the Centenary Year of St Teresa, but also in response to requests from readers who have long wished to see it reissued.

This most engaging and helpful book on prayer was written by a remarkable Carmelite friar, and it is with sadness that I have to say that Fr Jerome Lantry passed away on April 16, 2013. He was ninety-three. Originally from Ireland, he was an inspiring and kindly teacher at the Carmelite College of Castlemartyr, Cork, before being sent to the California region of the Anglo-Irish Province of the Order. He twice served as Provincial, and thereafter returned to Southern California where he would spend the rest of his life.

A true man of prayer, devoted to Christ, to the Church and to the service of others, he made a lasting impression on those with whom he came in contact, while never trying to put himself in the limelight. Quiet and unassuming, humble and kind, with a rare gift for the discernment of people, he strove to help and encourage others, which he did effectively by both word and example.

The present book contains both the word and the man: a compelling account of the teachings of his beloved St Teresa, conveyed with a quiet conviction that marked the life of the author and made his own teaching style so effective.

In *Praying with St Teresa*, he explores perhaps the most teaching-oriented of all the saint's works: *The Way of Perfection*. Written for her Carmelite sisters at their request, she introduces her readers to prayer – and to how to *live* a life of prayer – and also shares with us her spiritual commentary on the Our Father, which is widely considered to be one of the best, if not *the* best, ever written.

In his book, Fr Jerome opens up for us these two aspects of *The Way of Perfection*. In Part I, he discusses the most important themes and dispositions highlighted in St Teresa's teaching on prayer, and in Part II he explores her commentary on the Our Father, bringing out, with succinctness and directness, the main themes of Teresa's commentary – ideas which, if followed faithfully, have the potential to be life-changing.

As a pastoral man, the author has written a book that is direct, inspiring and always practical. With this in mind, I have added an Appendix containing 'exercises', so to speak, drawing on Fr Jerome's own words: lessons which he urges his readers to take to heart and put into practice – on a daily basis – because he knew from experience what the writings of Teresa gave to him personally, and because he genuinely cared about the spiritual life of his listeners and readers.

Surely Fr Jerome will watch over all who read this work, urging us to have the *will* to pray, and the will to do whatever God wants for us. In his original Preface, he said: 'This book presents St Teresa's teaching to anyone interested in prayer. By means of summary, quotation and comment, it puts *The Way of Perfection* within your reach.' To you who are reading this book now, those words are addressed to you.

James McCaffrey, OCD
Editor of *Mount Carmel*

Prologue
An Invitation to Prayer

In our times, so many, many people are turning to prayer in one form or another. This is great news, and there are lots of clear indications that this is not just a passing trend but something real. There is a search on today for something spiritual that is genuine and permanent. We have gone through so much change that we are wondering what is permanent and on what we can depend. St Teresa did some careful thinking about all that, too, and had a few thoughts which she wrote down and kept as a bookmark to keep her thinking straight. It said:

> Let nothing disturb you,
> Let nothing frighten you,
> All things pass away,
> God never changes.
> Patience
> Obtains everything.
> To the one who has God
> Nothing is lacking.
> God alone suffices.

Here we have some of the basic ideas that occur and recur in Teresa's writings. We can see that she had clearly decided that nothing is permanent and changeless, but God himself. Customs and laws, plans and structures can change, adjust or even disappear when they have served their purpose. New ideas grow old and give way to newer ones. People come and go, and even the indispensable ones move on. It takes time and thought to come to even a vague awareness of what St Teresa has written in her 'Bookmark'. People who find God in their lives find the one permanent thing there is, and they come to realise little by little that God fulfils all their needs – that God alone can do this.

It is this thought or intuition that draws people to pray. At first, they crave some sense of God that can be felt, and to which they react in an emotional way, whether in sorrow or joy or a blending of both. In time they learn to be aware of God in a much quieter and deeper way. They enter into a new world of truth and freedom, light and love. This is human life in full flower. People who find this way develop a great emotional balance, a deeper insight into life, and even a clearer intellect.

One other basic thing in St Teresa's life was her love for the Church. This may not sound that enticing to us if we have grown confused about the Church. If so, we are missing something very important and basic. The Church is not a building; it is not a highly structured and rich organisation.

10

The Church is the people. The Church came into being at Pentecost. The apostles, the people chosen by Christ as the first members of the Church, were all present but incapable of doing anything until the Holy Spirit came. Then they became new people, who preached fearlessly and continued to bring the faith to thousands in spite of being jailed, beaten and even banished.

This early group of Christians came to speak of themselves simply as the 'assembly'; the word 'church' is just a translation of that. This assembly, though, was in fact more than the group of people who were the members of it, which is equally true of us today. By a special gift of God, they were given a share in the very life of Christ, so that they were united to him, just as the parts of a human body share the human life that is in them, and as the branches of a tree share the life of the tree. This was brought home dramatically to St Paul at his conversion. When Jesus spoke to him, he said, 'Why do you persecute me?' (Acts 9:4). He did not ask why he was persecuting his *followers*. He did not make that distinction.

So, when we come to Jesus Christ in prayer, when we learn to pray, we are with God our Father and with his Son, who is not just my Redeemer and yours but the Redeemer of all people. Prayer is something we frequently do alone, just as Jesus did, but in prayer we are not turning our backs on people. Rather, we are reaching out to them.

Their welfare is our concern because it is God's concern.

St Teresa's awareness of God involved her more and more in the cares of the Church, but we must bear in mind that her notion of the Church was very personal: it was *the person of Christ*. In the members of the Church she saw Christ praised, served, persecuted, shamed, let down or glorified. Many times she spoke of a great wish to give her life and to give it a thousand times to save one human being from the consequences of sin. And this is exactly what Christ's life and death were all about – so we can, in a way, see the love of Christ for us reflected in Teresa's life.

Prayer brings us close to God and helps us grow in our love for him. So, *his* will becomes *our* will; and his will is that people, all people, should come to him. By knowing him and what he has done and is doing for us, we come to know our own worth and dignity. This is the way to peace and unity, the way to end crime and injustice and war. St Teresa was aware of these things, and was not turning aside but coming to help when she spent long hours in silent prayer – alone with God, her God and our God.

Teresa's love of Christ was a really beautiful thing. This comes out in the way she speaks of him. It is so very prayerful and human, sometimes mingling complaint with humour, joy with sacrifice, so much so that we keep on reading to see what she will say next. She speaks of Christ as a friend and companion, a loving teacher, a poor suffering man who must not be left alone, a great victorious king who has conquered a kingdom and wants to give it to us. Many times her instruction or narrative breaks off, and she is *writing prayer* – sometimes praising, sometimes pleading, but always so close to reality and so close to God.

It must have been this awareness of God's majesty and of our littleness that gave Teresa such a great sense of humour. It made her realistic about people, holding up to them the highest ideals and yet insisting on good sense and the acceptance of our limitations. She is certainly a most lovable saint. She seems to be saying so often, so persuasively: If it happened to me, why wouldn't it happen to you?

Part I
St Teresa on Prayer

Chapter 1
St Teresa's Writings

Prayer is the Theme

St Teresa was absolutely certain of the value of prayer in our lives, and she went to great lengths to teach and even coax people to pray. She did this not just for her own nuns but for all her friends, and that meant for many lay people and priests. This was her favourite gift. One might say that her way of saying: 'I love you' was: 'Let me help you to pray.'

She was a woman who was gifted with a quick mind and a most attractive personality. She made friends easily and summed up situations quickly. She was not easily satisfied, and in her relentless search she found God in prayer. Like the man in the Gospel who found the treasure in the field and who sold all that he had and bought the field, once Teresa found God in prayer she gave her life to this special field. It became her apostolate. Through this she supported the Church, sanctified its priests, spread the Gospel to new peoples, and lived the fullest Christian life anyone could hope to experience.

The story of her great life is told in her works. In a collection of her writings, you will find long books and short accounts of incidents in her life. You can find in these a good account of how she spent her years; but, first and foremost, those books are about prayer. They tell of prayer itself or of how she established communities dedicated to prayer, and the many negotiations this work entailed. Always the theme is prayer, and prayer is the purpose of her relentless effort. And all this because God is found in prayer and God is the only answer – the full answer to the multiple searchings of the human heart. No matter what you read by St Teresa, it will turn your mind to God: because she had come to that kind of friendship with God through which she was aware of him everywhere, whether she was happy or sad, busy or quiet. But there are a few books, in particular, to which people turn for instruction on prayer.

The Castle and the Garden

The one that is generally recognised as being her best is the last one she wrote: *The Interior Castle*, sometimes referred to as *The Mansions*. This book was written in 1577, five years before her death. The whole concept of the book is very close to the biblical teaching that we are the temples of the Holy Spirit (cf. 1Cor 3:16; 6:19; 2Cor 6:16). St Teresa speaks of the person at prayer as being a castle in which God lives in a central dwelling place or 'mansion' surrounded by six other mansions, each with its own apartments. The seven mansions represent stages of prayer, from the state of grace or being clear of serious sin (first mansion) to full mystical union with God (seventh mansion). The first, second and third mansions deal with the life of prayer we can develop by our own efforts with the ordinary graces God gives to all of us. The other four have to do with stages of prayer that can come only with special help from God.

The second book that is considered to be a main source of St Teresa's teaching on prayer is *The Book of Her Life*, sometimes referred to as her autobiography. A first version of this book was completed in 1562, but that account is lost. Teresa was later asked to rewrite it, which she did in 1565. Chapters 1-10 of this book tell of her early years insofar as they led to her dedication to a life of prayer. Then, in Chapters 11-22, she gives us a kind of booklet on what prayer is all about.

Here, Teresa speaks of the praying person as a garden or orchard which is made fruitful by being watered, and she tells us of four different ways in which the water comes. The water, of course, is God's grace, and so the four different ways of watering the garden are God's different ways of helping us to pray. The first way is to draw water from a well; this is prayer we can develop by our own efforts, so that it would be on the same level as the first three mansions. The second way of watering is to have a water wheel rigged up with buckets, so we can turn the wheel and draw so much more water with little effort. This is the beginning of a kind of prayer we cannot come to by our own efforts but only with the special help of God. Yet even here, we do contribute by being attentive to what he is doing and co-operating with his special graces. The third way of watering is an advance on the second: the water comes along in a stream which we just direct here and there. In prayer, this means we have less to do but still must co-operate in a smaller way. The final way of watering is simply by means of heavy rain, when the Lord does everything and we just enjoy his goodness.

For those learning to pray, both this section of the *Life* and all of *The Interior Castle* are worth reading. They are immensely helpful and instructive. Both were written in obedience to superiors who wanted Teresa's teaching on prayer, and we are most grateful to those men who recognised the value of her experience and were responsible for getting her to put so much of it for us in writing.

Walking the Path of Prayer

The Way of Perfection, however, was written for some of Teresa's own nuns who just wanted to get some help for themselves so that they could grow in prayer. So it is geared to getting people to pray and to instructing them on some practical matters that can help or hinder our progress in communicating with God. At first, the book was written like a long personal letter to a small group of nuns living with her. Later, when she saw it would be used in other houses, too, she rewrote it. This second version is the one that is normally used, but modern editions all include passages from the first version so that none of her thought is lost.[1]

The plan is simple and easy to pick up from the titles of the chapters – headings given by Teresa herself. She begins with a short Prologue that creates immediate interest because she tells us why she is writing the book: the nuns asked her to do so, she says, and because of their love for her the few things she has to say will be taken to heart by them. She also lists the sources of her experience: her life; her dealings with others; and what God has taught her in prayer. No doubt about it, she is writing from her own experience. When St Teresa began to encounter God's presence in very deep ways in prayer, she wisely went to a confessor for advice. Many failed to understand her, and she did not meet many who had similar experiences themselves. One of them asked her to write an account of what happened when she prayed. This was really the beginning of her writing.

Teresa was so clear in her description of delicate personal experience that she was often told to write. This description of things that would escape the attention of many is very interesting. It also makes for a personal style of writing that is full of real life. Chapters 1-3 of *The Way of Perfection* tell us why she founded a community given to prayer: to help the Church. Chapters 4-15 deal with three Gospel virtues essential to a life of prayer: love for one another, detachment from created things, and true humility. Chapters 16-26 deal mainly with contemplation, its ideals and demands.

Chapters 27-42 are Teresa's commentary on the Our Father. In themselves, they form a special work on prayer, from recollection to the prayer of union. Her plan is simple and her style personal, and it is no exaggeration to say that *The Way of Perfection* coaxes you to pray.

Chapter 2
A Strong Resolution

She Takes You by the Hand

Much has been said and written on prayer, and yet not many people seem to succeed in making prayer a way of life. The difficulty lies, to some extent, in the lack of resolution. This point is so important, so vital, that there is no way to highlight it too much. It is a known fact that St Teresa had a great problem in getting herself down to the daily practice of prayer, and we can see the struggle she had from her own words:

> very often, for some years, I was more anxious that the hour I had determined to spend in prayer be over than I was to remain there, and more anxious to listen for the striking of the clock than to attend to other good things. And I don't know what heavy penance could have come to mind that frequently I would not have gladly undertaken rather than recollect myself in the practice of prayer... After I had made this effort, I found myself left with greater quiet and delight than sometimes when I had the desire to pray. (L 8:7)

St Teresa is not alone in this teaching. Fulton Sheen made a Holy Hour every day and readily confessed that this was the fountain of faith from which he drew anything he had to offer. Fr James Borst tells how, after years of evasion, he got down to spending an hour a day in prayer, and that it felt so long he thought it was just stubbornness that kept him there.

This does not sound encouraging. It is not easy to grow in prayer, and yet we must begin and somehow we must succeed. Not to get down to the habit of praying is the biggest mistake we can make. We put it off and find alternative activities: we read, work, discuss, even pray in groups, go to lots of Masses and so on. All of these things are good, but they can be a hundred times better if we get down to silent, solitary prayer, alone with God. This is frightening, or at least something inside us says so, and we shun it. If you are an average good Christian, you have been shunning this for years. Frankly, you need help – and one sure place to find it is in a book St Teresa wrote for a small group of her friends: *The Way of Perfection*.

Time and again, she appeals to us to make up our minds once and for all: that, come what may, we are going to give time to quiet prayer; and no matter how dull, flat, dry-as-dust it becomes, we will go on and on. She calls not just for a resolution but for one that is strong; not just honest determination but the kind that is really determined. Do not think this is too much for you: because she will encourage, exhort, challenge, plead with and support you at every turn. This is what St Teresa does. She does not just instruct you in how to pray. She takes you by the hand and leads you to God and lets you stand before him – humble, grateful, glad to be there, reverent, afraid to offend but not afraid to receive and return love. To love God! Can you? Dare you? Is this your thing? Let her tell you.

God Loves Us

In *The Book of Her Life*, Teresa says this:

> mental prayer in my opinion is nothing else than an intimate sharing between friends; it means taking time frequently to be alone with Him who we know loves us. (L 8:5)

From this description and from the whole paragraph, there is evidence of a personal friendship built around the fact that God loves us and is waiting for us to respond. If you examine this carefully and find that this is the way you think, you are very lucky. Many people think of themselves as being unlovable in God's eyes, so that they are not at all ready to come near him in prayer. When St Peter first got an inkling of who Jesus was, he told Jesus to go away, and the reason he gave is still being used: 'I am a sinful man' (Lk

5:8). To be in sin and to tell the Saviour to go away, instead of asking him to come and cure us, is foolish; and yet, it is what we are doing every day. This 'depart-from-me-Lord' way of thinking has become so much a habit with us that we do not realise how often it triggers our reflexes and turns us away from anything that might have brought us face to face with God – our Father, our Creator, our Redeemer, our Friend.

St Teresa's idea of God as the one who knows all things, who can do all things and who loves us is worth thinking over at some length. It is good to hear, but we can too easily walk away and forget it. In order to learn what God is like, we search the Bible; and there, we see God first as the Creator of things. He is the Beginning, never created, never having to learn or grow in any way because he is perfect in every possible way. It is an easy conclusion from this that God is infinitely good. Goodness wants to give, and all creation is the result of God wanting to share his happiness. The living God who 'sleeps not, nor slumbers' (Ps 120:4) is vigilant, benevolent and all-powerful.

Three Pictures of God

The Bible tells us how God made a covenant with human beings like us. It was not usual for someone to make a pact of that kind with a person inferior to him, and for God to make such an agreement with the people he had created was a real revelation of his good will. As the people became aware of what God had done, we find the Bible expressing the story of the covenant in song, with all the language of high romance: it is the story of the King falling in love with the pauper. He is not put off by our unworthiness. This is what the Incarnation is all about. The song of the angels at Bethlehem gives this message: peace on earth to people who are the object of God's good will.

Every book in the Bible should be read in this light. For now, let us look at the fifteenth chapter of St Luke's Gospel. In that narrative, Jesus was criticised for being a friend of publicans and sinners and for eating with them. He replied by telling three parables illustrating the mercy of God. We are familiar with these stories of the lost sheep, the lost coin and the prodigal son. We have often thought about them, comparing ourselves with the sheep, the coin or the sinner.

It is well to reflect, though, that we also get three pictures of what God is like. He is like *the shepherd* who searches through wide, open spaces for you, for me. Why? Because we are his and we have strayed from him. He does not sit and wait to see if we will come back, but he leaves everything and comes to look for us. God is like *the woman who loses a coin*. She has nine more and is not in need, but the lost one is hers and she goes to look for it. This search is slow and careful, yet persevering and successful. The coin cannot come home of itself and yet is returned to its rightful place. And God, our Father, is like *the father of the prodigal son*. He waited and waited for the wayward one to come, and was filled with pity as soon as he saw him. That is a rare picture of God: an old man running out, through love for his sinner son who was lost and is found. These are not parables to be put aside; rather, they need to be put inside the heart and pondered frequently. We sinners are not servants but friends.

A Response to Love

God is like that: he hates sin but loves sinners, even while they are in sin. God does not wait for us to be good before he loves us. God loves us before we do a thing, long before we merit anything, and when we have nothing to offer. Our minds are like sick people trying to get back to health. They need good warm days and fresh air, and they need to sit or walk around enjoying the lovely weather. So, too, with God's love. We have to wait in it to be made healthy by it, to let it tan our entire attitude to things. It is the greatest of all mistakes to say to God: 'Depart from me.' We must correct that and say to him: 'Come to me, I will wait for you, I will find time alone to be with you. I will entrust my whole future to your love for me.'

God created you; he made you out of nothing. You were not and now you are. Isn't this an enormous commitment on his part? God made you and he will make something great out of you, no matter how you feel about yourself. Your sinfulness will not stop him. St John says this to us: 'God loved the world so much that he gave his only Son, so that everyone who believes in him may not be lost but may have eternal life' (Jn 3:16). He also says: 'This is the love I mean: not our love for God, but God's love for us when he sent his Son to be the sacrifice that takes our sins away' (1Jn 4:10).

If God loves you enough to make you out of nothing, and to send to Calvary his beloved Son in whom he was so well pleased, then our tendency to shy away from God is wrong, and lacking in faith and confidence. It takes time and work to reverse this trend, and yet such a change is necessary. It helps a great deal to talk to those who are aware of God's love, to read whatever brings it home to us, and in particular to search the Scriptures with the set purpose of learning this lesson from the Holy Spirit. St Teresa says prayer is an intimate exchange with him who we know loves us (cf. L 8:5). If we know this, we will find it easier to spend time alone with him – and to do this often.

Chapter 3
As We Live We Pray

Personal to Christ

A fundamental point in St Teresa's teaching is that life and prayer go hand in hand. This is very important and has some implications worth noting. We know from the Scriptures and all the teaching of the saints that, unless we are doing our best to carry out God's will and to live by our conscience, we are not giving God a chance to do all he has planned for us. What is especially interesting in St Teresa is the source of her information: personal experience. At the very beginning of *The Way of Perfection* she says: 'I shall say nothing about what I have not experienced myself or seen in others or received understanding of from our Lord in prayer' (WP Prol. 3).

It is also notable that Teresa says that the desire to change our ways comes from prayer; and that even if we fail to change, we should keep on praying and not give up, because we *will* ultimately change our ways. She also makes the very noteworthy point that if we hope to advance to real contemplation, we have to develop our way of living these three habits or virtues: *love of neighbour, self-denial* and *humility.*

At no time does Teresa quote the Gospel as the source for this teaching, so that it may well have come from her own experience. And yet, the three things she singles out as essential to contemplatives are the very same things which Christ emphasised as being in some way personal to himself. Of *love of neighbour*, he said that it was a new commandment, his commandment, the quality by which all would recognise us as his disciples. Of *self-denial*, he said that it was essential to following him, which is synonymous with living the Gospel. We must deny ourselves, take up our cross and be his disciples, his close followers. And of *humility*, he said: 'Learn of me that I am gentle and humble of heart' (Mt 11:29).

It is essential that we note how personal to Christ these virtues are. It is as if he were saying that he insists on them in his close friends. Nor is it a mere coincidence that we find them linked together in the document on the Church of Vatican II. We read: 'The Church, consequently, equipped with the gifts of her Founder and faithfully guarding his precepts of *charity, humility and self-denial*, receives the mission to proclaim and establish among all peoples the kingdom of Christ and of God.'[2] And it would seem that Christ taught these to St Teresa. Is it too much to suppose that he is more than willing to teach them to *us*?

In teaching these three virtues to her nuns, St Teresa takes lots of examples from day-to-day convent life, examples that would not always apply in other circumstances; but anyone who wants to grow in prayer, and who asks Christ for help with these essential qualities of living, will encounter practical examples every day. Take love of neighbour. St Paul, when emphasising the fact that love of neighbour is the greatest charism of all, says: 'Love is always patient and kind; it is never jealous; love is never boastful or conceited; it is never rude or selfish; it does not take offence, and is not resentful. Love takes no pleasure in other people's sins but delights in the truth; it is always ready to excuse, to trust, to hope, and to endure whatever comes' (1Cor 13:4-7).

All of the sixteen chapters of the First Letter to the Corinthians are worth careful study in the matter of prayer, to see what is permanent and what is not. But in particular, we can take a few points from the passage quoted and start to work on them day by day. Divide it into some *DOs* and *DON'Ts*. *Don't* be selfish, boastful, resentful. *Do* be kind, patient, forgiving, persevering. Try it – and the concrete situations will emerge. Out of this experiment you will begin to see in yourself some real failures in Christian living. Do not run away from them. The very fact that you can face them will make you a forgiving, tolerant person, slow to condemn and a good, patient listener. This is a solid beginning on which to build.

Real, down-to-earth love calls for generosity. Love really comes to life when it makes demands. This is the double line between using someone to love ourselves and really loving people for their own sake. St Teresa is very insistent on unselfish ways if we are to develop a life of prayer. In this matter of denying ourselves, as with charity and humility, she directs us repeatedly to compare ourselves with Christ and to learn from him. This makes sense. If we accept the fact that he lived his life and died and rose for us, then we will try to live for him and to be just a little like him in the way we live.

It is so easy to accept all this as a teaching and never put it into practice – which is just saying that it is right, but that it is really up to someone else to act on it. No, you must go with St Teresa to look at Christ in his Passion and to bring home to yourself that this special Friend went through all this for you. A young mother holding one child in her arms, and trying to save two more from being run down by cars, said to her own mother: 'I never realised you went through this with us.' This is the kind of 'realising' we need to do with Christ in the Gospels. This is what will bring out a response in our own lives, and the only way we can love God is by realising his love for us and responding to it. This is what St Teresa calls the 'current coin' (WP 18:7) for loving God. Not the high moment of mystical experience, but the doing or enduring of things unselfishly, so as to thank him for his splendid, unlimited sacrifice in which he loved us more than his own comfort.

The Freedom of Self-Denial

St Teresa reminds us of the good things God has done for us, and she calls on us to praise and thank him. There is great wisdom in this. We really need to count our blessings: then we will be able to find the hidden benefits in our trials, to list them clearly, and to thank him for them one by one. From here we can move on, into the fruitful field of things offered to God, and learn to let the grain of wheat die on the way to harvest. In this, too, we can learn from St Teresa, who advises us to make use of the trials that are already in our lives before we even think of doing anything beyond that.

There are many things we have to go without because we cannot afford them. This 'state of being without' is really a place where God is waiting for you. Compare your life with that of Christ. Did he have the thing you regret being unable to afford? Can you find consolation in the fact that you share this lack with him? Does it delight you? He loves a cheerful giver. From here, you will come to give to the poor for his sake. If Christ is our treasure and our heart is given to him, then the old human urge to make the million makes no sense, unless we gather it for his needy ones.

Material things, though, are not the only things that come between us and God. We get far too concerned about our health and comfort. St Teresa told her nuns to be 'manly' about such things and not to be preoccupied about small illnesses and unnecessary comforts. It is again a very personal matter that differs from one to another and from place to place. But look into the things you do every day, and see: are you over-concerned about health, or perhaps ruining it through lack of discipline? Here again is an area of self-denial, a place to compare yourself with Christ, to deny yourself in ways that will let him live in you.

Today we are more aware of our psychological make-up. Here again we find much to work on, things to change and things to live with, moods in need of attention and change, reactions and sensitivities that will not change unless we can talk to God about them. St Teresa is very strong on 'self-knowledge', and in her language this means something highly practical: we should note objectively how we act or fail to act, ask ourselves why, and try little by little with God's help to change. In the Scriptures, we see the Holy Spirit as one who removes 'impossible' barriers. It is a real sign of God-in-us to see some of our self-built walls crumbling and new freedom coming to flower. Without him we can do nothing, but in him we can do all things.

The final point in all this area is the surrender of our will to God's will. Teresa takes this up in many places and gives it a lengthy treatment in different books. She looks carefully at what Christ himself did and how he accepted the Father's will, even when he knew that this meant death. Then she says that when he taught us to say, 'Thy will be done', he was asking us to join with him in giving our will to the Father. Also, she reminds us that we are no heroes in this, but are just making a virtue of accepting and willing what is bound to happen anyway.

Resignation is not enough: we must give our will gladly and make sure that real action follows our promise. Not an easy matter but a very fruitful exercise: 'what strength lies in this gift! It does nothing less, when accompanied by the necessary determination, than draw the Almighty so that He becomes one with our lowliness, transforms us into Himself, and effects a union of the Creator with the creature' (WP 32:11).

Doing God's will is a truly great and Christian work and the sure test of all prayer. This is what is implicit in the words, 'By their fruits you shall know them' (Mt 7:16). But doing God's will is not all that simple. To expect to follow God's will at every turn can lead to scrupulosity. If you are keeping God's commandments, then what you are doing all day is good and pleasing to God. Just as we said about praying to him who we know loves us, so, too, we live our lives each day under the eyes of him who loves us and is pleased with all we do, so long as it is not sinful. This should help us to enjoy doing his will, even when it involves things not pleasant for us. This is the real secret of the saints: to enjoy doing things that are hard for us, in order to please him. Through these, we learn the real wisdom that comes from being close to God. There is no place we can get close to Christ so quickly as in his sufferings.

The Great Benefits of Humility

Obviously, this brings us face to face with our own weaknesses. We can see the truth about ourselves and yet not be discouraged by it. And this is what humility is all about. It is facing the truth while making sure the mood is right. To be able to come before God with all the respect due to him who made and redeemed us, and yet to trust in his goodness – this is the all-important basic lesson that makes growth in prayer possible.

Humility is a little subtle. We can think we are humble and yet be secretly proud. But there are some indications of real humility. Gratitude is one. To be aware of the goodness of God when things are going badly for us – that is humility. To see any good we find in ourselves as a gift of God, to want to be like Christ when he was accused and remained silent – that is his work within us. Teresa says: 'it calls for great humility to be silent at seeing oneself condemned without fault. This is a wonderful way to imitate the Lord who took away all our faults. So, I ask you to take great care about this practice; it brings with it great benefits. I see no reason at all for us to try to excuse ourselves, unless, as I say, in some cases where not telling the truth would cause anger or scandal' (WP 15:1).

It was only a great awareness of herself in the presence of God that could make her say: 'even though we are blamed for faults we haven't committed, we are never entirely without fault' (WP 15:4). For St Teresa, humility is the queen of all the virtues – by humility 'we will draw [the King] to our souls' (WP 16:2), she writes. But in fact, love of neighbour, self-denial and humility are so bound together in Teresa's thinking that they are inseparable. As she says: 'I cannot understand how there could be humility without love or love without humility; nor are these two virtues possible without detachment from all creatures' (WP 16:2).

Living the Virtues

All through her discussion of these virtues, there is a clear orientation towards the practical. They are not things to write about and explain, but something to do, like doing one's work. It is something planned and put into effect. 'We must all try to be preachers through our deeds' (WP 15:6), says Teresa. This is the key to the way her mind works. She exhorts, coaxes and encourages, and yet does not demand a standard or even a measurable progress. No, she wants practical, down-to-earth effort with a great honesty about ourselves. She will gladly accept our statement that we are 'no saints' but is very opposed to using this as a reason for not trying. As we live we pray, and as we pray we should try to live. It is not enough to give our attention to prayer: we must always be trying to give our life to God.

The great basic laws which call us to love God and to love our neighbour apply to prayer as well as to plain living. We cannot learn to pray just by getting hold of some techniques and putting them into practice. This may bring us calm and quiet and leave us with a clear, creative mind; but if it is not building a relationship with God who loves us, it is not prayer. If we can, time and again, pick ourselves up out of the dirt of our failures and keep on trying to make of ourselves an everlasting gift to him, we have something to bring to prayer. Otherwise, there may be some interesting experiences but they, of themselves, cannot kindle the fire of love; and prayer is an exercise in loving, even in the darkness of faith and the absence of hope. So, the surest way to build a life of prayer is to take up the instructions of him who teaches us to pray, and see how we do in putting them into practice – words of love, of self-denial, of humility:

> I give you a new commandment: love one another; just as I have loved you, you also must love one another. By this love you have for one another, everyone will know that you are my disciples. (Jn 13:34-35)

> If any want to become my followers, let them renounce themselves and take up their cross and follow me. For those who want to save their life will lose it; but those who lose their life for my sake, and for the sake of the gospel, will save it. (Mk 8:34-35)

> Come to me, all you who labour and are overburdened, and I will give you rest. Shoulder my yoke and learn from me, for I am gentle and humble in heart, and you will find rest for your souls. Yes, my yoke is easy and my burden light. (Mt 11:28-30)

Examine these words slowly and carefully. You will see that they are the words of a real friend

– one who put his life into what he said. Try to respond to these words. Without pretence, fully aware of your failures, begin to do what you can. He will give you courage and strength. You are taking the sure way to prayer.

Chapter 4
Learning to Pray

Drawn into Awareness

While we try to respond to Christ's call to love one another, and to give of ourselves and be humble, we also give time to prayer. We discuss these things separately, but in real life they form part of the same daily living. We need to learn to pray. We need to begin like the apostles by asking Christ to teach us to pray. It is the God who loves us who also teaches us to pray.

St Teresa sets about guiding us in prayer in a very simple way. She tells us to begin where we are. We have, no doubt, all been praying for years, and we may say we were just reciting prayers. But the fact is that we would not have gone on and on with them if they did not do something for us, and the something they do is to let us in some degree communicate with God. Teresa tells us to add some more *awareness* of what we are doing, and then we are on a sure road to a real life of prayer. Beyond that, she does not have a lot to say by way of technique. She tries to bring this new awareness into our prayer by telling us to ask ourselves three questions before we recite a vocal prayer: To whom am I going to speak? Who am I? What am I going to say?

Time and again in *The Way of Perfection*, she comes back to these three points. It is well worth your while to go to the Scriptures to look at people who spoke to God, and see the great awareness they had. In the Old Testament, there was Moses who was told to put off his shoes because the ground on which he stood was made holy by the presence of God. There was Samuel who said, 'Speak, Lord, your servant is listening.' In the New Testament, the relationship of Jesus with his Father is something to be studied and pondered. It is the most beautiful thing the world has ever seen. He was very much aware of his own humble state as man, and so always spoke with great reverence and yet with total love. The way in which he said, 'Father', 'my Father', 'righteous Father', shows a bond of great, great love and it is into this bond that he wants to draw you when he tells you to say, 'Our Father'.

We also have in the New Testament so many cases of people becoming aware of Christ, of the great unknown magnetic something in him. We see this first in Mary, who ponders it all in her heart, who shares his pain and is humbly grateful to be part of it. There are others, too: the centurion, Jairus, the man whose boy was a lunatic, the blind who saw, the deaf who heard,

the cripples – and even the dead – who walked
again, Mary Magdalene at the tomb, the apostles
in the upper room, Paul on the way to Damascus.
These people knew how to pray – knew that when
they turned to pray they were face to face with
Someone.

Face to Face with God

God is your Creator. Maybe you know a little of
the history of a hundred years ago. People were
busy with work, with special problems, with
much of what concerns us – yet none of us was
there. We simply were not. Now we are. We are
here – before God. He made us; he made us out of
nothing. So we stand before him in great humility,
remembering our origins, conscious of our roots.
And grateful. He saw us as possible persons and
made us actual human beings. He who is mighty
has surely done a great thing for me in bringing
me into existence.

Our first response in all honesty must be
adoration, but love goes with it. God made us
because of his goodness. It was a work of love, and
love is the response that expresses our gratitude.
When we look at ourselves and see how little we
are and how frequently we have failed, we soon
ask for forgiveness. This is the way, too, in which
Teresa asks us to proceed: to see ourselves as we
are, to examine our conscience, and to ask his

forgiveness. And she somehow makes it all sound like human politeness:

> If...others tell you that you are speaking with God while you are reciting the Our Father and at the same time in fact thinking of the world, then I have nothing to say. But if you are to be speaking, as is right, with so great a Lord, it is good that you consider whom you are speaking with as well as who you are, at least if you want to be polite. (WP 22:1)

Later, in the same context, she says: 'if before you begin your vocal prayer you do the great deal that must be done in order to understand these... points well, you will be spending a good amount of time in mental prayer' (WP 22:3). She is asking here for due attention to what we are doing when we say even the simplest prayers.

Obviously, this starting point in prayer is very important. It is the moment when psychologically we come face to face with God. It is a time to slow down, and to begin to do what the Psalm tells us: 'Be still and know that I am God' (Ps 45:11). This is a real moment of truth – truth that is at first frightening and then immensely reassuring. To come before him who made us is a mighty lesson in detachment from created things. It is, in this situation, incredible that we would prefer something created to him who created it. It seems so utterly foolish to turn our backs on him, thinking we can get more joy, more real happiness from what he has made than we could from himself.

A New Beginning

What a senseless thing, to be proud in the face of the fact that we came from nothing and are depending on God every second of our existence. How absurd to offend God when we are depending on him for the very energy to do so! To reflect in this way is real meditation. Indeed, all meditation should lead us back to the point where we stand face to face with God and know who he is and who we are. It is vital that we learn who God is and who we are at the same time. Trying to learn who we are without coming face to face with God is full of pitfalls; but in his presence we learn by a kind of deep intuition that we are because of him, that we belong to him, that he is committed to us and takes his delight in us. With this we become aware of our deep unworthiness. The guilt of our wrongdoing can be faced in this hallowed place. We know he knows it all, and that is something of a relief.

We hide this side of self from others, and we strive to hide it from ourselves. But if we stay still and hang on to this awareness of being face to face with him, we begin in time to become clearly aware of what we already knew in an obscure way: that everything within us is open to him. He sees, he knows, and we can say with real truth: I confess. We are aware not only of the trespasses we remember, but of a deeper unworthiness rooted in our inner being. And yet, he is right there in love and mercy telling us to come to him.

In order to bridge the great divide, he has become like me and has done what I could not do alone: he has made up for all my failures, paid my debts, brought me out of slavery, called me friend and child, and called me home. This is God. It is to him that I am going to talk when I pray. While we begin with a shivering awareness of ourselves – who we are, what we have done – we move on from there as we grow in confidence. The mercy of God is so beautiful; it lets us look at ourselves just as we are and still feel that everything is not lost, that there is a new beginning for us. We do not have to run away from ourselves. We are accepted as we are, and we are given room and opportunity to grow in his image in which we were first made. This is renewal, making all things new in us.

Chapter 5
You Before God

A Personal 'Way'

To come face to face with God in our own mind
– that is the beginning of mental prayer. Always
remember that God loves you. From here, there are
many ways to proceed. In *The Way of Perfection*,
St Teresa picks just one way and follows it through.
She works on the principle that if we say our vocal
prayers right, we are making mental prayer. So
she tells us to say the best of all prayers – the Our
Father – and to do it slowly, with some awareness
of God to whom we are speaking.

To take one method like this and stay with
it, until you have made a habit of it, is a very
necessary thing. When you read a lot about
prayer, about schools and methods of prayer and
about Eastern ways of deeper awareness, you can
fall into the trap of hopping from one method to
another. This is fatal because it prevents you from
acquiring the perseverance that is so necessary
in prayer. Prayer is a part of our life and has its
bright days and dull periods for many reasons.
No one has ever achieved anything in any field

without a lot of patience and real slogging. Many people have given up just when success was within reach, and so a great effort ended in failure. All our good resolutions about perseverance in prayer can be undermined by skipping from one method to another.

Those who stay with prayer finally come to a 'way' that is their own personal method; but in the beginning, it is vitally important to select one method and to stay with it. We do not necessarily have to choose St Teresa's method. Her virtue is not in criticising other methods but in following one and showing how it develops. In *The Way of Perfection*, Teresa takes vocal prayer as her starting point. In this there is much to draw on, and the prayers in the *Missal* and the Psalms, for example, provide excellent material.

Initial Dispositions

Teresa herself chose the Our Father, which is familiar to all Christians. This prayer was first given to us as a result of a request made by the apostles: 'Lord, teach us to pray' (Lk 11:1). So it is really *Christ teaching us to pray*, and we let him do this by keeping our attention on him when we say it. The first thing Teresa tells us, then, is to 'remember Him often when we say the prayer, even though because of our weakness we do not remember Him always' (WP 24:3).

The next direction is to be *alone* when we pray like this, which is something Christ taught us by example because he frequently went off alone to pray. This is no reflection on prayer in groups, but just saying that a life of inner prayer requires that, at set times, we do it alone. This requires some planning. We need to find the time and place. It is most helpful, if possible, to have a set time, place and posture for quiet prayer. This simple routine helps to clear the mind and to let our awareness of God come to life.

Here again, changing place, time or posture may give a brief 'lift' to our prayer for a while, but a patient *perseverance* with the one way of praying does more to deepen awareness. Teresa says: 'one cannot speak simultaneously to God and to the world' (WP 24:4). So we must do all we can to keep our full attention for him in prayer. There are also times when, for reasons we cannot understand, 'it can happen that God will permit days of severe temptation in his servants for their greater good' (WP 24:4). Even when things are calm, we do not often experience his presence but rather his absence. At these times, Teresa encourages us to persevere:

Do you think He is silent? Even though we do not hear Him, He speaks well to the heart when we beseech Him from the heart. And it is good for us to consider that He taught this prayer to

each of us and that He is showing it to us...
(WP 24:5)

God With Us and In Us

This point deserves a good deal of attention. If we come in quiet awareness to recite this prayer with attention to what we are saying (perhaps even whispering the words so that we can hear them), and we are also in a general way aware of God lovingly present with us, we come to sense that we are not saying it alone. When we pray, we are the heart of the Church and we breathe the very life of the Church. When we say the prayer Jesus taught us, it comes to us in some small way that 'the Spirit himself and our spirit bear united witness that we are children of God' (Rm 8:16). We are not alone when we pray to the Father. Jesus prays with us; or rather, we pray with him. The Spirit prays in us. We lend our breath to the Church when we pray. In one way or another, we need to bend our heart's attention to the fact that God not only calls and invites us to pray, but that Christ prays with us and in us.

It often takes an act of sheer faith before this is brought home to us, but it is still good to know that our prayer does not depend on our poor efforts. Nor is it impoverished by our wayward moods. To encourage us in this, St Teresa says: 'the teacher is never so far from his pupil that he has to shout, but he is very close. I want you to understand that it is good for you, if you are to recite the Our Father well, to remain at the side of the Master who taught this prayer to you' (WP 24:5). At other times, she speaks also of our Lord being *at our side.*

This way of thinking of God being present is not new. It is found in other writings and most notably in the Bible: 'The Lord is your guard and your shade; at your right side he stands' (Ps 120:5). It is quite possible that St Teresa found this here or in some other book, but she certainly made it her own and comes back to it at different times. It gives a setting for our communication with God.

A Companion and a Friend

When Teresa recaps her teaching up to this point, she emphasises this presence and makes it quite personal and very human:

> the examination of conscience, the act of contrition, and the sign of the cross must come first. Then,...since you are alone, strive to find a companion. Well what better companion than the Master Himself who taught you this prayer? Represent the Lord Himself as close to you and behold how lovingly and humbly He is teaching you. Believe me, you should remain with so good a friend as long as you can. If you grow accustomed to having Him present at your side,

and He sees that you do so with love and that you go about striving to please Him, you will not be able – as they say – to get away from Him; He will never fail you; He will help you in all your trials; you will find Him everywhere. Do you think it's some small matter to have a friend like this at your side? (WP 26:1)

That passage is worth reading time and again. The impression of Christ that comes through from it is surely one that makes you want to know him as a *companion* and a *friend*. Many times Teresa pleads with us to make this awareness of him a habit – and tells us to stay with it until it becomes a habit we would not think of breaking. She tells us to ask him to be with us; and if we go a whole year without acquiring the habit, she still wants us to go on and on trying, and not to grudge the time because there is no better way we could spend it.

In telling us to go on trying to form this habit, she says it is not necessary to have great thoughts or deep insights:

I'm not asking you to do anything more than look at Him. For who can keep you from turning the eyes of your soul toward this Lord, even if you do so just for a moment if you can't do more? (WP 26:3)

To urge us on again, she says we can surely look at 'the most beautiful thing imaginable' (WP 26:3), and she reminds us that Christ never takes his eyes off us, even when, because of our sins, we are not that pleasant to look at. So, surely, it is no big thing for us to turn away our attention, sometimes, from other attractions and to look at him. It is really a matter of making up our minds to do this. 'In the measure you desire Him, you will find Him' is the way Teresa says it. Just try and he will help you: 'He so esteems our turning to look at Him that no diligence will be lacking on His part' (WP 26:3).

Any Place, Any Time, Any Mood

To give a further push to our effort, Teresa gives us the example of how a wife tries to please her husband and adapt herself to his moods. We do not have to do this with God: for he is the one who adapts himself to *our* moods. This is an excellent human way of getting across the very important principle that we do not have to put on appearances before God; we do not try to be someone else or even to change our mood. We start where we are and he comes to us there; and where he leads us is his business. One author has said it so well: 'Every man has his own secret trail to God. Any soul, at any time, in any place can enter into communion with its Maker. There is no influence or permission necessary to gain admission to the Presence. No matter how estranged and outcast, every man can leave the barren country at a moment's notice and come at once to his Father.'[3]

We can indeed turn to God in any place at any time. But to do so requires real faith. So very, very often we fail to make this effort of faith that could do us so much good. This is the little pressure that opens the secret door to the hidden treasure we have passed by for so long. The hardest part of praying is to begin. But people who have acquired the habit of giving time regularly to prayer would find it harder to give up than to continue. So whatever the mood, let us not put off the practice of turning our attention to God and letting the eyes of our mind rest on him. St Teresa gives us an example of how to pray when happy or when sad:

> If you are joyful, look at Him as risen. Just imagining how He rose from the tomb will bring you joy. The brilliance! The beauty! The majesty! How victorious! How joyful! Indeed, like one coming forth from a battle where he has gained a great kingdom! And all of that, plus Himself, He desires for you. Well, is it such a big thing that from time to time you turn your eyes to look upon one who gives you so much? (WP 26:4)

That passage is worth rereading, for it will help us to become more and more aware of what God is like. At great pain he has won for us all we need, and he is delighted. Are we? And if we are sad, St Teresa has this to say:

> behold Him on the way to the garden: what great affliction He bore in His soul; for having become suffering itself, He tells us about it and complains of it. Or behold Him bound to the column, filled with pain, with all His flesh torn in pieces for the great love He bears you; so much suffering, persecuted by some, spat on by others, denied by His friends, abandoned by them, with no one to defend Him, frozen from the cold, left so alone that you can console each other. (WP 26:5)

And she goes on to say that in comforting us he will forget his pain, because we have come to accompany and comfort *him*. This blending of your suffering with Christ's Passion is the very best thing you can learn in prayer. This is what Christianity is about: to come to the point where, like the apostles, we can rejoice to have been found worthy to suffer something for him.

A Real Transformation

This sounds like a high ideal, very far from where we are, but there simply is no Christian alternative, and even the weakest beginning will grow in strength. So it is very wise, when you experience trials, to take them to him in his sufferings; and if you can do nothing else, tell him how much you are hurting. Walk the road to Calvary with him. Take that passage from St Teresa, just quoted, or any meditation like it, and start to turn it into your own words until you are saying *your* thoughts, making *your* meditations, having *your* conversation with Christ; until *your* pain is joined to his, and you feel his love for you in his sacrifices for you, and you begin to respond and to see that you are not suffering because of your sins or because God does not care, but because he *does* care – because he wants to pull you up into life with himself on a closer level.

His resurrection and our eternal happiness are the final story, and we must always rejoice in the hope this gives; but the here and now is a time of trial in which we need to know the lessons of the Passion. Look for a saint who did not lean on the Passion for strength, and you look in vain. You need your own meditation on the Passion. Every life is a fresh insight into the life of Christ, and each new trial tells us new things about his death and resurrection. In time, your meditation will be refined into a simple thought and expressed in a short prayer. But in the beginning and occasionally later, it is good to express it in detail.

Through this prayer you learn to stumble and fall *with* him, not alone, and to love the cross and see it as a blessing. This is a real transformation. If you still need to be convinced that the cross is the sure way to deep prayer, then read Mary Craig's *Blessings*. Here you will meet many people who found new depths in living through the heavy trials life gave them. And St Teresa asks you to look at Mary Magdalene and Mary, the Mother of Jesus, and to see how they stood with him in his Passion – and so learn from them that this is the way to go.

Teresa tells us to practise enduring small trials, and to get a picture of Christ and talk to him about them until this becomes a habit. She insists we can do this. Technique is *not* the big thing; but the will to pray, to get close to him often, until it is a habit, until it is your life – that is the real thing. She also suggests using a book that helps you to pray. She did that for years. Try every way you can to stay at his side. To grow accustomed to this, to make it a solid habit, is what makes a real, unbelievable difference in life. This is the place of opportunity; it is where gold is found, where life begins at any age and goes on eternally. Everyone lives by the habits they have formed, habits of doing and of not doing. If you are like so many others, you have a habit of not coming close to God, of not being caught alone with him. It is time to change that; it is time to make his friendship and companionship a way of life – of new life.

Part II

Praying the Our Father
with St Teresa

Chapter 6
'Our Father'

A Beloved Parent

To pray is to come face to face with God in all
honesty and humility, yet in confidence as one
coming home to a beloved parent. From this
position it is easier to call God 'our Father'. This is
the very beginning of prayer as Jesus taught it, and
St Teresa has much to say on this. Many excellent
things have been written on the subject of God as
our Father, beginning with the Bible and going on
still. The theology here is deep and will never be
complete. St Teresa's comments are not those of
a theologian or scholar but come from her own
lived experience, and this is a very helpful guide
for us in developing our personal relationship
with God, our Father.

Those who, like St Thérèse of Lisieux, had a
special relationship with their own father are off
to a good start, but even those who were not so
fortunate can find here immense compensation and
develop unused resources in themselves. History
shows that God has revealed his fatherhood in the
lives of all sorts of people. He can do all things.

What we think we are or have been is no obstacle to him. So we can look at what St Teresa has to say, with a readiness to believe that, while that is personal to her, there is something in us, too, that is ready to respond to God, our Father, if we give ourselves the time and opportunity.

Prayer begins when we come to ask who God is. And the first word in the answer is 'Father'. This word is a revelation of what God is like and how he feels about us. It is certainly an invitation to come to him and to stop acting like a stranger. It invites us into heaven itself. And that is Teresa's first reaction.

With the Father and the Son

Teresa also sees how much it tells us about Christ: as Son of God, he is now made a brother to us and comes to live with us, no matter what our state. The very thought of this turns her from her ordinary style of writing to a prayerful address to Christ in which she marvels at what he has done: he has given us everything at once, joined in the prayer of us sinners, and so obliged his Father to accept us as his children, to pardon our sins, to comfort us in trials, to sustain us as fathers do and more than they can, and finally to share with us the right to inherit all his possessions (cf. WP 27:2).

That is a beautiful passage that brings to mind some words from St Matthew: 'I bless you, Father,

64

Lord of heaven and of earth, for hiding these things from the learned and the clever and revealing them to mere children. Yes, Father, for that is what it pleased you to do. Everything has been entrusted to me by my Father; and no one knows the Son except the Father, just as no one knows the Father except the Son and those to whom the Son chooses to reveal him' (Mt 11:25-27).

St Teresa does not refer to this Scripture passage, and yet her very first words of comment on the Our Father are certainly in close harmony with it: 'O my Lord, how You do show Yourself to be the Father of such a Son; and how Your Son does show Himself to be the Son of such a Father! May You be blessed forever and ever!' (WP 27:1). And there is one more point worth noting. When she turns to speak to Christ on this same matter of his telling us to call God 'our Father', she is amazed and delighted that Christ should 'humble [Himself] to such an extreme in joining with us in prayer' (WP 27:2).

Rooted in this Eternal Bond

Immediately after the passage from St Matthew just quoted, we find Christ saying: 'Come to me, all you who labour and are overburdened, and I will give you rest. Shoulder my yoke and learn from me, for I am gentle and humble in heart' (Mt 11:28-29). St Teresa goes on talking to God,

65

marvelling at the fact that he is giving us so much by making us his own children, and finding no explanation except that he so loves to give that no obstacle can stop him. One other reflection of hers says that he is doing this to make us love to learn what he is teaching us. Finally, she says that, rather than write more about it, she will leave it to us to think about.

This is a matter deserving repeated attention at length. Here is the very centre of your life, the home from which you go out and to which you return. Of its very nature, this relationship with God, your Father, links you to Christ, your Brother, and to all people as your own family. St John had grasped all that very clearly when he told us of what he had seen and heard, so that we would share it all with him and be together with him in union with the Father and his Son, Jesus Christ.

Since St Teresa finds in the opening words of the Our Father a real revelation of what God is like, it seems appropriate here to quote the opening of the document of Vatican II on Revelation, as it too lets us see the loving way in which God makes himself known to us: 'In his goodness and wisdom, God chose to reveal himself and to make known to us the hidden purpose of his will by which through Christ, the Word made flesh, people have access to the Father in the Holy Spirit and come to share in the divine nature. Through this revelation, therefore, the invisible God out of the abundance of his love speaks to people as friends and lives among them, so that he may invite and take them into friendship with himself.'[4]

It yet remains for each of us to come before God and live out our own relationship with him, in such a way that it may grow – and all we think and do will be firmly rooted in this eternal bond.

Chapter 7
'Who Art in Heaven'

In the House of our Heart

The words of the Our Father 'Who art in heaven' bring St Teresa to deal directly with the subject of *recollection*, the practice of withdrawing our attention from outward things to focus on God within us. So she very logically concludes that we have no need to go to heaven to find him, nor to speak in a loud voice to be heard by him. All we need is to find a place where we can be alone and just look at him who is present within us. He is within me in the house of my heart and I can come in humility and confidence and talk to him, ask him for things, tell him my troubles, beg him to set things right for me, and yet not fail in my reverence for him.

Here, St Teresa has something to say about people who will not come close to God on the grounds that they are not worthy, and she tells us to avoid this foolish thinking. She does not say so, but such an attitude may contain an unwillingness to come close to God: because closeness to God, of necessity, makes us aware of our sinfulness and calls on us to repent. St Teresa encourages us to face this by letting us know that he will teach us how to please him.

The message is clear: the Lord is within us, and we should be there with him. This being within ourselves is prayer that Teresa calls 'recollection': 'because the soul collects its faculties together and enters within itself to be with its God' (WP 28:4). A special advantage that she sees for the soul in this type of prayer is that 'its divine Master comes more quickly to teach it and give it the prayer of quiet than He would through any other method it might use' (WP 28:4).

St Teresa herself had experienced prayer of a kind that cannot be achieved by our own dedication or by techniques, but only by a special grace of God. While she tells us time and again that we cannot reach such states of prayer by our own efforts, she is particularly anxious that we should dispose ourselves for this special grace. Indeed, she seems as sure as she can be that we *will* receive this special grace if we make a habit of recollecting our mind in prayer and persevere in the practice. She says this is like travelling by ship with a favourable wind as opposed to walking. You get there so much faster.

Genuine recollection can be known by the effects it has on our way of living. It brings out in us a serious effort to do things God's way. All of which is based on the Gospel teaching that where the treasure is, there the heart goes (cf. Mt 6:21). As the heart turns more and more to God within, it ceases to be drawn by things that had attracted it so far. As the habit grows, the eyes are closed in prayer as an outward expression of where the interest is centred. The effort to be recollected has to be a strong persevering one, but with practice it becomes much easier; or perhaps it is more correct to say that the effort gets strong as the habit grows. The wish to enter into recollection comes to harvest. This is the world in which the will to sin weakens and the fire of divine love is enkindled: because we are alone with him and he is close to us.

Some people are confused as to how to imagine God close to us – before us, beside us, within us, or just close to us. Teresa does not see any problem. The place she speaks of as 'within us' is a vast space, a palace of great beauty, incomparably more precious than anything we can see. In it is a special place reserved for our Guest, and this place is our heart.

Later in life, when her understanding of all this was deeper still, Teresa returned to the idea and called her finest book '*The Interior Castle*'. Here, she speaks firstly of the soul as a heaven in which God delights. The inner beauty of a life lived for God is, she declares, too beautiful to be described. Then she goes on to speak of the 'mansions' of *The Interior Castle*, and in so doing describes with great clarity seven stages of prayer. So it is possible to be in this castle with our Lord, and still to be striving to get close to him. The reason is that he does not reveal himself to us in the beginning but has gradually to prepare us for each new understanding of himself that he wants us to have.

This is a slow process which we can help along by striving honestly and generously to give ourselves to him more and more in the way we live out each day. The wish to please and serve him and not ourselves is the secret way to deepen our prayer. St Teresa says we should empty the castle so that he can put in and take out whatever he wants. This sounds lovely but it calls for a lot of detachment.

And yet God gives the strength, the moment we make the effort. This makes us review our whole set of values until we come more and more to prize the things that last and forget what passes. Values become very much eternal values, and much of what we have valued highly now seems insignificant. This change of heart and outlook is an immense help to prayer. It opens the way for

God to work in us, and to make us ready for the gifts he has for us. It is plain to everyone that, before God, we are very small; if he were to make us suddenly aware of his presence, we would be terrified and he would have to reassure us.

Preparing for his Coming

It is obvious, then, that to prepare for his coming we should have a clear idea of just how small we are in his eyes. Indeed, if things happen that make us feel small, we should be glad of them and reflect how close they bring us to the truth. This, too, prepares us for his gifts. St Teresa says:

> It is better...that you be unappreciated and humbled, and that you accept this for the Lord who is with you. Turn your eyes inward and look within yourself, as has been said. You will find your Master, for He will not fail you; rather, the less you have of exterior consolation the more He will favour you. (WP 29:2)

St Teresa returns to a combination of urgings and instructions to help us acquire the habit of recollection. She begins by emphasising the importance of desiring it, since it is not something we have to wait for but something we can acquire by our own repeated efforts. She does not expect a lot of us in the beginning: 'Although it may be for only a moment that I remember I have that Company within myself, doing so is very beneficial' (WP 29:5); 'we should see and be present to the One with whom we speak without turning our backs on Him... All the harm comes from not truly understanding that He is near, but in imagining Him as far away' (WP 29:5).

It is so very obvious, every time she comes back to this, that there is work to be done. We must make the effort to get our mind off other things and onto him who is here, near us. It is only with frequent trying that this practice will grow into a habit. It is one more example of the truth of the axiom that where there is a will, there is a way. It is a matter of wanting the greatest thing we can have, and of being wise enough to want it badly. One sure result is that we will come, in time, to realise that he is aware of what we are saying, that he is listening to us as we pray. This makes us say the prayers more slowly, and even stop saying them so as just to be there, aware of him and knowing he is aware of us. This may not last for long, but it is the goal we are trying to reach; to arrive even for a little while is a great achievement.

From these moments of awareness, things we once knew from our own meditations take on a new light, as if they had just been taught to us in a new way. God teaches us to be still, to know that he is near and that he loves us, and he invites us to respond. So, by saying our vocal prayers well, we can grow in this awareness of God within us, loving us, caring for us – God who made us, God who redeemed us, God who changes us until we are like him. This is a simple, sure way with little room for error. Do it often, and do not give up. The habit may be acquired in a year, but we should be willing to work longer. The very effort has its own rewards.

God's Greatest Gift to the Soul

The emphasis on effort, gentle but persevering, is very much a vital part of St Teresa's teaching. For those who have experienced the benefit of recollection, the reason for this is clear; but for the beginner it may not be so obvious. Teresa's purpose, her objective, is union with Christ. He is the one she is seeking, and he is so important to us that the desire to reach him, to come close to him, should be so strong as to be worthy of him.

In the beginning, when the person trying to pray has so little to work on, it is important to be convinced that, at the end of this search, there is the most precious treasure we can possibly find. Prayer is where God reveals himself to us individually, and his greatest revelation is his Son, Jesus Christ. He is God's final and clearest Word. All other forms of revelation receive fresh light from Christ. We get to know the Father through him; it is his Spirit who is sent to sanctify us. So in the world in which we live, he is the one to attend to. The Father said: 'Listen to him.' We 'hear' and 'listen' and attend by coming to him in recollection.

The impression of Jesus Christ that we get from St Teresa is one of immense good: a Person who is loving, merciful, generous, humble, patient, and yet strong and unafraid. All this may be distant from the beginner, but it becomes clearer as we practise recollection. We may have nothing to say, other than the words of prayers we have learnt; but if we say these slowly, they begin to relate to our life and then to his. It may not be easy to focus our attention on him. We may have to try to picture him in ways that will make it easier to keep our minds on him. But if we are convinced that he is our wealth – our gold mine, so to speak – we will go on and not give up.

So, the strong desire of the heart to come to Christ is vitally important. A habit of prayer is something to strive for throughout a lifetime. It is God's greatest gift to the soul. Prayer consecrates us and makes us holy and pleasing to God; it makes us walk the earth with a freer swing, not as slaves of the world but as people who are free in Christ.

Litany
of the
Holy Spirit

LITANY OF THE HOLY SPIRIT

God, the Father in heaven	have mercy on us
God the Son, Redeemer of the world	have mercy on us
God the Holy Spirit	have mercy on us
Holy Trinity, one God	have mercy on us
Holy Spirit, proceeding from the Father and the Son	have mercy on us
Spirit of eternal truth	have mercy on us
Spirit of wisdom and understanding	have mercy on us
Spirit of counsel and fortitude	have mercy on us
Spirit of knowledge and piety	have mercy on us
Spirit of fear of the Lord	have mercy on us
Spirit of grace and prayer	have mercy on us
Spirit of love and power	have mercy on us
Spirit who in the beginning moved over the waters	have mercy on us
Spirit by whose inspiration the prophets spoke	have mercy on us
Spirit who overshadowed Mary	have mercy on us
Spirit who descended upon the Son of God at his baptism	have mercy on us
Spirit who appeared over the disciples at Pentecost	have mercy on us
Spirit by whom we are all born to the spiritual life	have mercy on us
Spirit dwelling in us as in a shrine	have mercy on us
Spirit guiding the Church	have mercy on us
Spirit converting sinners	have mercy on us
Spirit making the faithful but one heart and mind	have mercy on us
Spirit giving your children true liberty	have mercy on us

Chapter 8
'Hallowed Be Thy Name, Thy Kingdom Come'

Invited to the Eternal Vision of God

We now move onto the first petitions of the Our Father: 'Hallowed be thy name, thy kingdom come'. St Teresa's comments on them give us a fine example of what she means when she tells us to think of what we are saying when we pray. In this case, she reflects on what we are asking for in our petitions; she also recommends that we ask for light, so that we may see the implications of what we are requesting. And she sees these two petitions as inseparable: unless God's kingdom comes in us, how can we ever rise to praising his name?

Teresa argues from what we hope to be doing in heaven, in the perfect kingdom, to what we should be doing now, in this kingdom:

> Now, then, the great good that it seems to me there will be in the kingdom of heaven, among many other blessings, is that one will no longer take any account of earthly things, but have a

calmness and glory within, rejoice in the fact that all are rejoicing, experience perpetual peace and a wonderful inner satisfaction that comes from seeing that everyone hallows and praises the Lord and blesses His name and that no one offends Him. Everyone loves Him there, and the soul itself doesn't think about anything else than loving Him; nor can it cease loving Him, because it knows Him. And would that we could love Him in this way here below, even though we may not be able to do so with such perfection or stability. But if we knew Him we would love in a way very different from that in which we do love Him. (WP 30:5)

This may be regarded as a personal interpretation of a Scripture text. But it leaves no doubt that prayer, attention to God, is no academic exercise but a real act of loving God – a way that is personal, committed, and free from contrary attractions. The experiences of interior prayer are an invitation to the eternal vision of God. What St Teresa is saying can be more readily understood by bearing in mind that the 'kingdom of God', as we know about it in the synoptic Gospels, can be said to apply both to heaven – the perfect kingdom to which we look forward in hope – and also to the kingdom among us which we identify with the Church, the new people of God. The kingdom among us, which we also call the Mystical Body of Christ, is found in people. We say that Christ is the head of the Church, his Body, because it is his life in us that makes us members of the kingdom here, and heirs to the kingdom we seek.

Aware of his Presence

Given that we share in some real way in the life of Christ, he is made present to us, to the extent that we can know him by faith and love him with a degree of the same love which comes to perfection in heaven. By recollection, we become aware of his presence in us: sometimes by a passing experience that lets us feel his action in us, but much more frequently by faith which lets us know that he is here even when what we feel does not convey such a message. This presence of God as experienced mainly by faith alone is what St Teresa has in mind when she thinks of the kingdom we want to come. This is not a departure from the usual meaning, which sees the petition as a prayer that asks for all people to come to believe in Christ: because, for St Teresa, interior prayer touches the heart of the Church and is very definitely apostolic and contributes in a vast way to the spread of the Gospel.

As God reveals himself to us in prayer, he is making his kingdom come in us and is enabling us to praise his name. When we say these petitions, then, we are not just asking that other people in faraway places come to do as we do, but also that we wake up to what God is doing and make room for him to live in us, in a way that we will be more aware of him and he can reveal himself to us more and more. This calls for dedication and unselfish love and, at first, a willingness to be upset by his presence which can make us uncomfortably aware of our own faults.

This growth of awareness of God within us brings St Teresa to describe a state of prayer in which God intervenes in our efforts to focus on him and gives us an awareness of himself that we cannot bring about by our own efforts. This does not happen suddenly but in a very subtle way, so that the first signs of it that we notice are not things that happen in an instant but things that come gradually and amount to a change in our way of praying.

Attending to an 'absent' Lord

If we have developed recollection as a habit of prayer, then we come to a practice, with some variations, whereby we bring ourselves to an awareness of God as someone close – a Friend who listens, a good Companion, even though he is silent. Then this awareness begins to change, until the method that makes us sure he is with us leaves us with a sense of his absence. We try again with the same result. We cannot get the reaction we got before. We cannot pray as we did. This happens even when there is a great desire to communicate with God and no wish to fix our attention on anything else. Not that our thoughts may not wander to other things. They may do; but even then, there is an anxiety because God is somehow 'absent', 'gone away'.

This 'absence' goes on and on for a long, long time. It is accompanied by a fear that we may have caused it, and so it gives rise to a great desire to do anything God wants and not to offend him. It is a difficult time and yet a very beneficial time. The only kind of prayer we are capable of now is a kind of attention to God that is very real but impossible to describe, as there is 'nothing in it'. It is a kind of blind attention without any kind of detail that we can describe. Yet it gradually brings its own satisfaction. At first it brings the awful fear that we are doing nothing, and this is a very testing time; but if it brings the fear of offending God and an agonising wish to 'find' him again, then it is most important we keep it up – just attending to this 'absent' Lord in loving attention that is dark, blind, and devoid of feeling or thoughts that tell us anything.

We have been given a new and higher way of communicating with God, and our first impressions for quite a while are just an awareness of the old ways that have gone out of action. But a new light has come; and our silent, anxious, attentive fidelity will turn the winter into spring and the first snowdrop will lead to a garden of flowers. This transition from a way of prayer we had established with long, patient practice, and from some earnest work on doing things we thought were God's way to a way we had not known about, is a difficult time and one that needs help and direction. But it is good to know of it and to be ready to persevere in it if God grants it to us. St Teresa so frequently exhorts us to persevere in prayer that it is obvious that the life of prayer, by its very nature, must call for this resolution to continue at least at certain times. And this is one of those times when continued practice of one way of praying is vital.

Real Humility

Prayer is so definitely a gift of God that it is most helpful, and conducive to real knowledge of ourselves, to be left helpless at times. If we jump from one way of praying to another, we do not stay long enough in one way to experience long enough our real inability to pray. This experience over a lengthy period develops in us an awareness of our spiritual poverty, which we will not forget when the Lord grants us higher things. This is vitally important.

What we gain from this experience is real humility. In spite of what we think, we get proud of our success in prayer. We give up things, discipline ourselves, and come to some success in that we are able to pray and have a sense of achievement. But when it all changes, we want to switch to something else that will give back that sense of achievement, a sense of being in control of the situation. St Teresa insists that it is by means of our humility that God is led to give us the new way of prayer which cannot come about without a special intervention on his part. While we hope and pray that God will grant this to us, while we strive to prepare and dispose ourselves for it, we must not strive to produce it or to 'practise' it. Our hope must never rest on our worthiness, which would be building on sand, but on the loving goodness of God, who is the rock on which the wise one builds.

Hence the importance of boundless trust and unfathomable humility. We keep our mind on God whom we do not see. The pilgrim's journey is one of faith. Even when certain things reassure us of God's presence, we must not cling to them but always focus on God, whom we do not see as long as we live. When faith and trust and humility have grown as evidence of our sincere, generous love, then God lets us know that he is there in the dark. The 'absence' is found to contain the 'presence'.

Passive Recollection

This new awareness comes very delicately at first and more discernibly later. The first stage is often called 'passive recollection', in the sense that it is a form of recollection in which our attention is somehow 'caught' or controlled by God. In *The Interior Castle*, St Teresa says that when people are fully convinced of the importance of prayer and have been practising recollection:

> the great King, who is in the centre dwelling place of this castle, sees their good will, He desires in His wonderful mercy to bring them back to Him. Like a good shepherd, with a whistle so gentle that even they themselves almost fail to hear it, He makes them recognise His voice and stops them from going so far astray so that they will return to their dwelling place. And the shepherd's whistle has such power that they abandon the exterior things in which they were estranged from Him and enter the castle. (IC IV:3:2)

This is St Teresa's description of the first awareness of God's special gift of what we call 'infused' or 'passive' prayer. She comments further:

> Don't think this recollection is acquired by the intellect striving to think about God within itself, or by the imagination imagining Him within itself. Such efforts are good and an

excellent kind of meditation because they are founded on a truth, which is that God is within us... But what I'm speaking of comes in a different way. (IC IV:3:3)

This is very interesting. It comes naturally from this truth: that we are dealing with something we cannot produce, either by thinking or imagining. Even for those who never come to this stage, it still provides great insights into God and gives a glimpse of how far his ways and thoughts are above ours. We sometimes feel great fervour in our prayer, at least on special occasions such as retreats, pilgrimages, and feast days. This emotion could also be aroused by a national event or the return of a friend or a dramatic performance. The fact that it is directed to God in prayer is a great thing, but that does not make it anything more than a lovely human feeling brought about by human means in a religious atmosphere. The Shepherd's call is different in its cause and source. As Teresa writes: 'it doesn't come when we want it but when God wants to grant us the favour' (IC IV:3:3).

Our Response to the Gift

Teresa gives us some guidelines on how to react to this favour. One obvious thing is to praise God for so great a gift. Then we should not strive to reason it out, to master it or grasp it with the mind, 'so that the soul...strives to remain attentive and aware of what the Lord is working in it' (IC IV:3:4). Teresa is speaking here of attention to and awareness of God. We attend to person and action, not to thought. To get the idea that we should 'go blank' in order to let this prayer develop is not correct:

> without any effort or noise the soul should strive to cut down the rambling of the intellect – but not suspend either it or the mind; it is good to be aware that one is in God's presence and of who God is. (IC IV:3:7)

Again, this piece of advice is very valuable to all of us. If at this stage, when God's special action is already evident, we rightly do not try to help it on by blanking out our mind, then it makes no sense to do that at an earlier stage in prayer. There are a number of things we can do to create the right atmosphere for prayer and dispose ourselves for a proper loving attention to God, but the whole purpose of all this – giving our attention to a loving God – is ruined if we just go mindless.

Another observation by St Teresa is of interest. At this stage, people experience a great freedom of spirit. Because of the new way of loving God, there is a stronger resolve not to offend him. This resolve finds expression in the careful avoidance of even the risk of offending him. There is a certain confidence of coming into his eternal presence, an anticipation of his welcome that draws us away from whatever is not pleasing to him. And for anyone engaged in meditation, such thoughts are valuable; they are the kind of thoughts that coax us to pray.

The Prayer of Quiet

Now to return to the Shepherd's call. It is the first signal that the person is coming into a stage or area of prayer that is called the 'prayer of quiet'. In *The Way of Perfection*, St Teresa is somewhat hesitant to talk about this: as she senses that some of those for whom she was writing would not believe that this would ever happen to them. She comes to this in the thirtieth chapter where she is commenting on the petitions of the Our Father, 'Hallowed be thy name, thy kingdom come'.

Teresa gets into her subject carefully and, we might say, slyly. She says that unless God's kingdom comes within us, we will not be able to praise his name. So she takes a quick look at what it must be like in heaven, so as to get across the point that we must work for and expect some change within us, if we are to aspire to that blessed stage. Then she admits the objection that one would need to be an angel to reach that state. She answers this by telling the story of a person who knew no other way to pray than to say the Our Father and yet, through that, was led by God to pure contemplation. So, the conclusion is obvious:

if we are going to say the prayer he taught us with the care it deserves, it is possible that he will teach us things we could never have learnt on our own.

And so to the prayer of quiet. All the phrases Teresa uses bring out the fact that it is a gift of God:

> the Lord begins...to show that He hears our petition. He begins now to give us His kingdom here below... This prayer is something supernatural, something we cannot procure through our own efforts. In it the soul enters into peace or, better, the Lord puts it at peace by His presence... (WP 31:1-2)

The person who is praying realises that God is very close; he or she feels great reverence, experiences the greatest delight, keeps still.

Giving us a closer look, though, Teresa says that the functions of the mind are changed. She says that the understanding, imagination and will are stilled – quietened to the point where they are more attentive than they could ever have become by their own efforts. The understanding and imagination enjoy a greater realisation of God's presence, but they are still free to attend to other objects. The will is captivated, not to the point of losing its freedom, but by giving itself unreservedly to God:

> The will is the [faculty] that is captive here. If there is some sorrow that can be experienced while in this state, that sorrow comes from a

realisation that the will must return to the state of being free. (WP 31:3)

Persons in this state like to remain motionless, speaking is distressing, they spend a whole hour on a single petition of the Our Father. No more is necessary now. God is so close that any little sign expresses all their love. Sometimes tears come, but without sadness. Joy, delight, praise of God – this is everything.

The Will Clinging to God

This 'captivity' of the will sometimes shows itself outside prayer time. For a day or two, the person in this state can work and attend to business without being fully involved, because the strong new bond with the Lord goes on even outside prayer. St Teresa says the person is like Martha and Mary at the same time.

Teresa follows her description of the prayer of quiet with a warning that we cannot bring it about, and that an anxiety to hold onto it could disturb the peace it brings and so upset it. Yet it does help to use a word or gesture to renew it if it is weakening. She then tries to show that this is not the highest form of prayer. She says this is like a child being fed and having nothing to do but swallow its milk. The 'prayer of union' will be like having the milk placed in the child's stomach with no effort at all on its part.

Again, this kind of prayer, even when we just read about it, tells us a lot. While the will is firmly clinging to God, it is possible for the thoughts and imagination to run wild. So in our ordinary prayers, the will to pray may be quite strong while the mind will not settle and we suffer continuous distractions. What we regard as good prayer or successful prayer is usually the prayer that brings us satisfaction. Such prayer is beneficial, but the final test is the degree to which it pleases God, and how it binds our will and heart to him; and this is known only to him. Prayer that brings consolation should be pleasing to God, our Father. Prayer that tests and increases our generosity is always a delight to him.

Chapter 9
'Thy Will Be Done...'

The Wisdom of the Saints

What we can learn from St Teresa's descriptions of the prayer of quiet is that what the heart and will are about is more important than what is going on in the mind or emotions. And this brings us easily to the next petition of the Our Father: 'Thy will be done on earth as it is in heaven.'

St Teresa starts out by telling us not to be afraid to offer ourselves to God so as to let his will be done in us. In her own humorous way, she reminds us that, in the end, his will *is* going to be done if we are to come to any good – so we are not all that generous in telling God to do it his way! 'I am amused by persons who don't dare ask for trials from the Lord,' she says, 'for they suppose that in doing so they will be given them at once' (WP 32:3).

People may shy away from asking for trials out of humility. They know themselves and realise they are too weak to bear trials. This is very honest as far as it goes, but God gives strength to bear the trials he sends. And the source of this strength comes from our Saviour who, in order to give us this strength, suffered more than he will ever ask of any one of us.

This is the way to eternal life, and we save ourselves a lot of anguish and time if we face it firmly and put our hearts into our prayer when we say: 'Thy will be done.' This is not just resignation – it is real, willing, generous love of God. This is where love blossoms and grows. To do God's will, to stay with his commandments and let the pain involved happen in silence, even to seek ways of giving things up for him, to be ready to suffer in silence as a secret way of loving God – this is the wisdom of the saints. This is the heart and soul of prayer, of loving God.

Finding Love in Adversity

What our heavenly Father did to his beloved Son is impossible to understand. He sent him to a painful death. No human father would think of doing such a thing. God's ways are not our ways. And his way of suffering is God's way of loving something in our sin-laden condition which makes it necessary that it should be so. God's mercy is his greatest work, but his justice had to be satisfied so that our dignity could be restored.

It is good to recall the case of Abraham who was told to sacrifice his only son. And he set out to do just that. Abraham, here, was a revelation of God the Father. It was as if God were saying: 'Can you do what I have to do?' And Abraham's readiness made him worthy of this call. In the end, he did not have to make the sacrifice, but he had to be ready to make it. He had the wisdom to know that God's will must be done. We can see how St Teresa shows the same insight:

> Well, see here...what He gave to the one He loved most. By that we understand what His will is. For these are His gifts in this world. He gives according to the love He bears us... And He gives according to the courage He sees in each... I myself hold that the measure for being able to bear a large or small cross is love. (WP 32:7)

So, prayer is not just another of the games people play. We cannot make a mockery of God by just promising what we do not mean to perform. Deeds must match words, and failures must lead to new effort. This is what makes for sincerity, honesty, integrity and real love. This petition also leaves us open to whatever God may send us. When we find his love in adversity – and it is often more difficult to find it in small things – it is more refined and more lasting. This, it seems, is the secret wisdom of the saints.

The Key to Deep Prayer

The gift of our will to God, then, is the real key to very deep prayer:

> what strength lies in this gift! It does nothing less, when accompanied by the necessary determination, than draw the Almighty so that He becomes one with our lowliness, transforms us into Himself, and effects a union of the Creator with the creature... And the more our deeds show that these are not merely polite words, all the more does the Lord bring us to Himself...so as to make [us] capable of receiving great favours... His Majesty never tires of giving. Not content with having made this soul one with Himself, He begins to find His delight in it, reveal His secrets, and rejoice that it knows what it has gained and something of what He will give it. He makes it lose these exterior senses so that nothing will occupy it. This is rapture. And He begins to commune with the soul in so intimate a friendship that He not only gives it back its own will but gives it His. (WP 32:11-12)

This is about as far as St Teresa goes in describing the development of passive prayer in *The Way of Perfection*, but she covers this whole area at length in *The Interior Castle*, and those who need such knowledge can study it there. Here, she passes on, having warned us that we cannot come to these heights by our own efforts and that attempting to do so achieves nothing except to spoil the kind of prayer that we are able to make: 'if you try to reach it, the devotion you have will grow cold. But...simplicity and humility...will achieve everything' (WP 32:14).

This prayer of union is a long way from the simple beginning where we give a little thought to the prayers we say and ask ourselves who it is to whom we are speaking, who we are and what we are saying. Yet it is no more than a God-given deepening in love of that original position. Anyone can see how wise St Teresa is in telling us to begin prayer – and continue it – with a simple awareness that brings us face to face with God. It is so different from trying to act in a way that will impress others, or from attempting to create any special reactions within ourselves. God alone teaches us to pray, and we let him do that by giving him our attention. We are, after all, responding to him – to his love, to his revelation of himself, which is his Son, Jesus Christ.

Chapter 10
'Give Us This Day Our Daily Bread'

The Highest Gift

Teresa's commentary on the union of our will with God's is magnificent, but perhaps too high for us. And she realised that, too. So, in her commentary on the next petition of the Our Father, 'Give us this day our daily bread', she says that our Saviour knows our weakness and how difficult it is for us to keep our promise to do his Father's will. Keeping this promise is vital, and so he must find a way for us to do so in spite of our weakness. The way is simple and yet too great to expect: he will stay with us himself and he will be our strength. He is our daily bread, given to us each day by his Father – *our* Father.

While this is true of every way in which Jesus is present to us, St Teresa applies it here to the Eucharist in particular. She is amazed at this evidence of God's love for us. The manner of his presence hides all his power and leaves him at our mercy. He can be despised, forgotten, insulted;

and yet he is there and will stay as our food to give us the strength we do not have – to be our strength so that we, who could do nothing of ourselves, can now change our ways and do the Father's will because of his Son who strengthens us. When we ask God for our 'daily bread', we must not waste our time over passing needs but ask for the highest gift God is offering – his divine Son – that he may live in us and enable us, with him, to do his Father's will. To do all things to please God, not to please ourselves, is real freedom. It allows us to put all our anxieties and worries in God's hands, and to rely on him to take care of them for us. This may come easily to some, but for many it has to be renewed daily.

For Healing and Faith

When St Teresa gets down to the specific help we receive from the Eucharist, she begins with the Blessed Sacrament's *healing powers*:

> Do you think this heavenly food fails to provide sustenance, even for these bodies, that it is not a great medicine even for bodily ills? I know that it is. (WP 34:6)

She then goes on to tell us about a person she knew (she was actually speaking about herself) who was immediately cured of serious illness and great pain through the Eucharist. This is of particular interest in our time when the belief in healing through prayers has revived. We have the special case of the anointing of the sick for their cure, rather than for a happy death. A cure through prayers and trust in God is also part of this sacrament. All such cures come through the power of God, the same power that Jesus used in the Gospel and that Peter invoked to heal the cripple at the entrance to the Temple. The fact that we are left a sacrament of healing means that this is a standard part of the Church's ministry. So it is proper for us to expect such effects from the greatest of the sacraments, the Eucharist.

Next to this, St Teresa speaks of *faith* coming through the Eucharist as she prays that we might receive it 'in such a way that the Lord may reveal Himself to the eyes of our soul' (WP 34:5). We also need to strive to strengthen our faith before we receive him. Today we are familiar with what we call the 'Liturgy of the Word' at Mass. This is the use of Scripture readings and reflection on them to strengthen our faith and so prepare us for receiving the Eucharist. This is the way that Teresa went, too, because, as she says, again speaking of herself, she 'strove to strengthen her faith so that in receiving her Lord it was as if, with her bodily eyes, she saw Him enter her house. Since she believed that this Lord truly entered her poor home, she freed herself from all exterior things when it was possible and entered to be with Him' (WP 34:7).

A Sure Way to Contemplation

This brings us right back to recollection, to finding God within us. It is obvious that we can think of God being within us after we have received him in Communion. Not only can we do this at the time: we can recall the memory of it at *any* time, and be helped to become familiar with the fact that God lives in us. St Teresa goes on to say:

> She strove to recollect the senses so that all of them would take notice of so great a good, I mean that they would not impede the soul from recognising it. She considered she was at His feet and wept with the Magdalene, no more nor less than if she were seeing Him with her bodily eyes in the house of the Pharisee. And even though she didn't feel devotion, faith told her that He was indeed there. (WP 34:7)

This makes the Eucharist a sure way to contemplative prayer, and the subject brings St Teresa back to a point she made previously, telling us that God is here and not away off in a distant heaven:

> In Communion the event is happening now, and it is entirely true. There's no reason to go looking for Him in some other place farther away... why doubt, if we have faith, that miracles will be worked while He is within us...? (WP 34:8)

And the important miracle is to obtain the courage to do God's will. But he is so approachable now in this humble disguise that we do not have to lose courage at the sight of repeated failures but can always begin anew. Even the person who has fallen time and time again can have a fresh start. Christ is here for our benefit and is willing to begin with the very weakest.

Winning the Inner Country

It is important to bear in mind that Christ is present to us in the Eucharist in a special way. We call it 'sacramental', and a sacrament is a visible sign given power by Christ to produce in us some spiritual effect we could not produce of ourselves. Baptism has a sign of being drowned and rescued, or of being dead and coming to life, and its effect is to give us a new kind of life for the first time, a sharing in some way in the very life of God. The other sacraments increase this and, if it is lost, Penance restores it.

Now the Eucharist is a sacrament under the sign of food – bread and wine – so that its effect is a strengthening of existing life. All of which means that, when we receive our Lord himself as a sacrament, all the time he is present he is feeding us with new life and giving us the strength to do what was not possible before. Christ is present not just to comfort, console and heal, but to *strengthen* us so that we can do his Father's will as he did, make a new beginning, and set out with firm resolve to do something good and beautiful so as to bring joy to our Father in heaven.

When we receive Jesus Christ, the Son of God, the full payment for all sin, there is no limit to the changes that can take place between us and our Father. We know that lifelong habits will not break easily, that old ways do not change, and that miracles are not to be multiplied. It is true that long-standing habits can reduce the scope of our freedom; but where there is no freedom, there is no fault, and God alone knows us as we are. He can leave us our weaknesses and busy himself with our inner selves – our deeper lives where we are still free and fully capable of doing good and avoiding evil – and can win that inner country for his Father. The world of the sacraments is a whole new world, linked with ours and yet above it. Nowhere do we receive its impact more fully than in the Eucharist.

At Communion time, we are really back to the fountain of life. The answer to all our needs is here. So we call out to God for help and we spell out our needs. But we must bear in mind that he knows a whole lot more about our needs than we do. So there is a lot of wisdom here in just giving our attention to him and letting our wonder and love grow in the strength of his presence – in the light of his love for us. It is such a still time, full of the dawn. 'Be with Him willingly; don't lose so good an occasion for conversing with Him as is the hour after having received Communion' (WP 34:10).

Here is the perfect situation for him to teach you some of the inner meaning of the Our Father. But for that, he needs our attention – and as a matter of habit. We must 'stay with him', be with him, recall him, come back to him – until he is in reality the centre of our living, the home in which we are fed and loved, from which we go out and to which we return.

Chapter 11
'Forgive Us Our Trespasses...'

The Will to Forgive

St Teresa proceeds to another petition by showing the logic of her reasoning up to now. The big thing for us to accomplish is to do God's will. We cannot do this with our own resources alone. So he gives us strength for the task: our daily bread. So, now we can begin, we can come before God ready to do his will – but being in his presence makes us again aware of who we are and what our record is and our condition. So we promptly ask to be forgiven our sins.

The way in which our Saviour tells us to do that is by teaching us to say, 'Forgive us our trespasses as we forgive those who trespass against us.' St Teresa is fully aware of the deliberate linking of our forgiveness with others: of God forgiving our sins, and of us forgiving all who offend us. She points out that the petition indicates an existing practice and not just a good resolution. We who crave forgiveness are forgiving in our own lives.

It is God's will that we forgive each other, so this practice is actually one of the things we are praying for when we say, 'Thy will be done.' When we forgive, then, we are doing his will. That is why, as Teresa says:

> the saints were pleased with the wrongs and persecutions they suffered; they then had something to offer the Lord when they prayed to Him. (WP 36:2)

From this idea, she draws some hard conclusions: that she herself has nothing to forgive; that instead of being blamed unfairly, she is not blamed enough, because people do not realise how sinful she is. So she says her forgiving is not worth anything, and that it most certainly cannot pay for the forgiveness she is asking of God. By implication, the same goes for you and me.

This brings her back to the old question of our honour, of standing on our dignity, of nursing a grudge instead of being humble and forgiving in the face of our own need for understanding and mercy. If we are to come close to God, then we have to begin to be like him, and the place to begin is here: to forgive so that we may be forgiven. We are not losing our reputation, for our true honour is to be found in God's salvation of us, not in a passing reputation. St Teresa says clearly, with detachment from her own concerns: 'Others will look after me if I forget about myself' (WP 36:5).

All this is also clearing the ground for a fuller love of each other. If we join our will with God's will, then we want what he wants: not the death of the sinner, but that the sinner be converted and live. We want goodness and joy and peace and unity. God wants us to be like that. He does not want us to be in opposite camps, fighting over rights or possessions: 'how important it is for us to love one another and to be at peace' (WP 36:7).[5]

This may seem rather idealistic, but St Teresa is speaking from the experience of union with God, a form of prayer in which the will is united to God's will without reserve. In the light of this experience she is able to speak with real authority. In fact, she frequently stresses the fact that trials and crosses are good for us at this stage, and that being slighted by others helps us to grow in this union with God. It brings a great sense of eternal values, so that all passing things are noticed less and less. Instead of looking for praise, such people are anxious to be seen for what they are, which is another example of what the merciful Lord is doing for a sinner.

Here is a quotation to remember: 'the resolve to suffer wrongs and suffer them even though this may be painful...will soon be possessed by anyone who has from the Lord this favour of the prayer of union' (WP 36:11). If this kind of fortitude does not begin to show itself, then any special states of prayer are suspect. So fortitude is a sure sign of the work of the Holy Spirit. He can manifest himself in many ways; but if he is making us holy – making us like Christ – and letting Christ live in us, then a courageous love of the cross will appear. And this is surely a good principle to apply in proper measure at any stage of prayer.

The Our Father has its own special insights for people very close to God, but it is also the special prayer of all of us. In it, each of us can express our individual needs and say what we want to say. We do not have to rise above ourselves to pray, but simply see ourselves as we are and speak honestly and truthfully to God. When we say the Our Father in this way, we see in the words the meaning that matches our lives, and the words we use begin to affect the way we live. This is real prayer. As Teresa writes:

> if...our actions and our words are one, the Lord will unfailingly fulfil our petitions... It must be realised, however, that these two things – surrendering our will to God and forgiving others – apply to all. True, some practise them more and some less... we will do what we can, and the Lord will accept it all. (WP 37:3)[6]

Chapter 12
'Lead Us Not Into Temptation'

Walking Before God

We pray to God, our Father, to lead us not into temptation but to deliver us from evil. Each of us can list some of the temptations and evils we want God to keep away from us, be they persons, places or things, and it is good at times to repeat this petition quietly and to mention each of the things we have in mind. This helps to bring our prayer and our day-to-day circumstances together; it makes prayer more real and life more prayerful.

From her experience, St Teresa tells us how to apply this petition to our life of prayer. She repeats the very important fact that prayer and the cross work closely together, so that it is far more important and infinitely wiser to face up to trials than to be looking for consolations. When our prayer is fervent, it is very important to be humble about it and remind ourselves that we are not worthy of this. A great sense of God's generosity and our own unworthiness is what we need when our devotion is strong.

A bigger danger is in thinking we have certain virtues when we don't. This leads to pride, and pride goes before a fall – and before we know it we have, as St Teresa says, 'sprained our ankles' (WP 38:5).[7] This piece of advice should not be looked upon as just a handy rule of thumb. In fact, it is one application of an overall attitude that is absolutely necessary in spiritual matters. We like to grade our progress, to see how we are doing, and we do this in order to encourage ourselves. In this frame of mind, we tend to look for signs of progress and to invent or exaggerate them. This is a wrong approach with a very dangerous result. The result is that we put ourselves in an unreal situation, a role for which we are not prepared, and we go from one error to another. It is like a person who is not physically fit getting into games. He can very easily sprain an ankle.

When we are dealing with spiritual matters, the mistakes of judgment are not all that obvious. This is an icy surface and we have to be alert to keep our balance. The basic mistake here is in comparing ourselves with others or with our own performance at a previous time. This kind of comparison is good if it makes us humble, but once it begins to give us satisfaction we must go back to the really valuable comparison by which we come face to face with Christ. We begin to pray by placing ourselves before God. In every way we can, we should return to this most important basic position.

When the Bible speaks of walking before God, aware that he is looking at us, it is putting us on the right path. When we turn from God, we are in danger of putting on appearances, acting a role, wearing a mask; but before God we know we have nothing that we have not received, and from that beginning we can grow up as people of God. If we watch our day-to-day behaviour, we learn that actually we are very changeable people. The strength we experience on a certain day may be gone the next day; and the assurance which carries us through a whole decade may desert us and leave us without the courage to tackle any situation. St Teresa said this happened to her so regularly that she came to see that whatever virtue she had was just on loan; she is particularly anxious that we take heed of that lesson.

The Truth about Ourselves

God has to keep us humble, because this reflects what we are. If we hold onto this truth, he can give us the virtue we need when we need it. If we make the mistake of thinking that the courage or detachment God has given us is something we have acquired and now own, he must leave us without this ability so that we come back to the truth about ourselves. This is the sort of thing we may observe easily enough in another, while we fail to see what is happening in ourselves. God gives each new day, and we use it all in his service. The next day we ask again for everything we need to serve him, and for that alone.

To stay before God and develop a deep, permanent sense of how small we are is real wisdom, and so we pray to God to keep us in this frame of mind and to save us from any temptation to change that. St Teresa goes on to point out the difference between thinking we have some virtue and actually being tested in a concrete situation. This, too, may seem obvious but it can so easily escape the notice of the person to whom it is happening. It is very easy to think that we are people who forgive and are free from prejudice, until we are put to the test. When God sends us trials, it is most important that we notice the good they do us and thank him for that. Not so easy but very Christ-like.

At certain times in history, one virtue or another comes into style and it is fashionable to be seen to practise it. In such an atmosphere, everyone speaks a certain language in praise of work, peace, helping the aged, or whatever is being promoted at the time. This is good in itself, but the individual may just be speaking the language while avoiding the concrete actions which the real situations require. Real, solid virtue looks for action, not just for words or feelings.

There are many subtle mistakes whereby we can deceive ourselves and think we are serving God when we are just trying to please ourselves. We need God's guiding hand in this strange world of goals and motives. It is an area through which he must shepherd us, and so we pray: 'Lead us not into temptation.' As Teresa says: 'The truly humble person always walks in doubt about his own virtues, and usually those he sees in his neighbours seem more certain and more valuable' (WP 38:9).

This living in humility, in honest truth, before God is a great healer of anxious hearts. It should bring us, slowly but surely, to realise in actual living that we are completely dependent upon God. We worry about possessions, about friends, about our health, and perhaps even more about our reputation. It is a very good thing to talk to God and tell him just what worries us and why. If we keep doing this, we are bound to begin to see that he controls all the things about which we worry. We are anxious because we are not in control – we must learn to be happy that *he* is in control. This is a difficult lesson to learn, and yet we cannot afford to live without it. It is a real sign of trust in God's love for us, a sure test of how deeply we believe in that love. 'Stop worrying about yourself and leave God to provide for you, come what may' (WP 38:9).[8]

Learning to See the Truth

St Teresa has a final word on humility, and it is to warn us against a type of it that is not genuine. If people come to know the value of humility and try to deepen it in their lives by coming frequently face to face with God, there is nonetheless something to be avoided in this valuable practice. It is the danger of dwelling on past sins and concluding that we are not worthy to be close to God. That could drive people from prayer and even from the sacraments; but, in less severe cases, it could still undermine our confidence in God's love for us.

There is something in us that keeps telling us God is not interested, is not close, does not care, or that all the good things we hear about God's merciful understanding do not apply to us due to some known or hidden fault in us that makes us unworthy. We do not, mercifully, follow this complex to its logical conclusion where we say our sins are too great to be forgiven; but we settle for a middle line which says that we are not good enough to be given any special call from God or to develop a deep friendship with him. Humility certainly makes us aware of our sins, but this awareness does not disturb or distress us: rather, 'it comes with peace, delight, and calm' (WP 39:2).

Here St Teresa gives a very valuable piece of advice, and all who feel they do not belong close to God should take it to heart and put it into practice regularly:

> When you find yourselves in this condition, stop thinking about your misery, insofar as possible, and turn your thoughts to the mercy of God, to how He loves us and suffered for us. (WP 39:3)

This is a very helpful rule for many people whose confidence in God is too weak to be worthy of him. It is a practice that will grow in us until we are lifted out of the mire of fear and we begin to love God.

When we come to this new experience, we should be glad of it, and yet not develop another wrong self-image. The same persons who for years made the mistake of thinking they were somehow unclean and just not fit for God's love can now substitute a sense of sinlessness that is again far from the truth. This leads to minimising real faults and lowering moral standards, at least in some matters.

This needs to be watched, as it can lead to real sinning; it can draw the unsuspecting into real sin. It is substituting a new sense of freedom for the reality of being face to face with God. If we can, in all honesty, tell God that we are doing something to please him and do not believe it is against his will, then all is well. If we have doubts, we should consult a confessor or friend who we know will tell us the plain truth. As Teresa points out:

however many delights and pledges of love the Lord gives you, never proceed with such self-assurance that you stop fearing lest you fall again; and be on guard against the occasions of sin... (WP 39:4)

Our Saviour has taught us to pray to our Father in heaven, asking him to steer us clear of temptation. In her reflections on that, St Teresa shows us some of the mistakes people make when trying to practise prayer. In so doing, she becomes aware that such warnings could lead people to conclude that it might be safer not to do too much praying. So she hastens to correct such thinking. She says that people who say the Our Father sincerely will not go astray: 'Prayer is a safe road; you will be more quickly freed from temptation when close to the Lord than when far' (WP 39:7). And that surely makes a whole lot of sense.

Chapter 13
'Deliver Us From Evil. Amen.'

The Big Request

The final chapter in *The Way of Perfection* is on the concluding words of the Our Father, 'Deliver us from evil. Amen.' St Teresa's reflection on this is very much that of a saint: to her, it was a request to be delivered from the misery of this life and brought immediately into the everlasting joys of heaven.

She says that Jesus prayed for this because his life was so full of suffering. She herself asks for it because she is only a sinner and getting worse instead of better:

> I do not find [a] remedy [for imperfection and sin] while living, and so I ask the Lord to deliver me from all evil forever. What good do we find in this life, Sisters, since we lack so much good and are absent from Him? Deliver me, Lord, from this shadow of death, deliver me from so many trials, deliver me from so many sufferings,

deliver me from so many changes, from so many compliments that we are forced to receive while still living, from so many, many, many things that tire and weary me... (WP 42:2)

This eloquent outburst may be beyond our own reactions, but it is worth our while to reflect that we must pass on from here and that no one has seen, heard or even imagined the good things awaiting us. This exercise of joyful hope is a great way to become detached from all the things we cling to with a mere finger-hold. Also, when we ask to be delivered from evil, we are not asking to be free of all pain and to endure nothing in God's service. We ask to be free of offending God and then to serve him in a state of sacrifice and joy.

Ultimately, we are asking that, in the end, heaven will be ours and we will be saved from all evil. It is the big request that we should make with confidence. We are talking to God who can give us anything and wants with all his heart to give us everything: 'What does it cost us to ask it, since we ask it of One Who is so powerful? It would be insulting a great emperor to ask Him for a farthing' (WP 42:4).[9]

'From the mouth of Truth itself'

Here, this unique commentary on the Our Father ends. But Teresa still has a few things to emphasise:

118

Here you see, friends, what it means to pray vocally with perfection. It means that you be aware of and understand whom you are asking, who it is that is asking, and what you are asking for. When they tell you that it isn't good to practise any other kind of prayer than vocal prayer, do not be distressed. Read this very carefully, and what you do not understand about prayer, beseech the Lord to teach you. For no one can take vocal prayer from you or make you recite the Our Father hastily and without understanding it. If some person should take it from you or counsel you to give it up, do not believe him. (WP 42:4)

In this short passage, we can hear a whole lot of echoes of things said before: the value of praying frequently, in honest simplicity and alone with God who loves us. Teresa is amazed at all that is contained in the Our Father, so much so that she feels we do not really need any other method of praying and can even get on without any further instruction apart from what is to be got from this prayer:

when books are taken away from us, this book cannot be taken away, for it comes from the mouth of Truth itself, who cannot err. (WP 42:5)

And so, we have come to see that prayer is not the achievement of the highly skilled or of those trained in techniques. It is the gift of God to anyone who believes in his love and speaks to him humbly, sincerely, frequently, and with the faithful perseverance that love requires. It is possible for you and me. The question is not: Have I been called? But: Am I resolved to answer the call? The answer comes today, not tomorrow. Today means yes, tomorrow means no. The concluding words of *The Way of Perfection* remind us that it is a very good thing to praise God frequently:

> May the Lord be blessed and praised; from Him comes every good we speak of, think about, and do. Amen. (WP 42:7)

Epilogue
The Twin Gifts of Love and Fear

Honest Thinking about Ourselves

Just before St Teresa discusses the final petition of the Our Father, she summarises a good deal of her advice by saying:

> what His Majesty gave us are love and fear. Love will quicken our steps; fear will make us watch our steps to avoid falling along the way. (WP 40:1)

And she begins to explore what we might call an 'inseparable pair' along the way, on our journey to God.

When St Teresa or any saint speaks of the fear of God, they are not talking of a scrupulous fear, or of fear such as that experienced under the rule of a tyrant. No, it is a fear of offending God, which is actually an expression of our love for God. It is a sure sign that we genuinely love him.

Knowing our ability to sin, we are afraid – not just because of the wrath of God that it might bring, but because we genuinely love God; and as a practical development of that, we do not want to offend the greatest Friend we have. We are naturally afraid, but the correct way to handle fear is to focus it on what is *really* to be feared.

If I am afraid of God because I know he can punish me for sin, that is a healthy fear, and when higher motives do not appeal to me it will keep me from offending him. The desire to please God contained in this kind of fear is practical and somewhat self-centred, but it is still to be highly respected and was taught by Jesus himself. That is just applying good common sense to the eternal implications of our actions. The motivation is not perfect; but nonetheless, it is rich and to be commended.

As this healthy fear of God becomes refined, it is concerned with not offending God *because of his goodness*. When Jesus said, 'I always do what pleases [my Father]' (Jn 8:29), he gave us a perfect standard to follow. He did not say, 'I *try* to do what pleases my Father.' No, he always did it, and without fail. He was human like us, except in one area: he was without sin.

We work from a basis of being redeemed sinners. So we come to the work of pleasing our loving Father with the knowledge that we have within us the ability, and even the inclination, to offend him; indeed, we have a history and habit of offending him. So our fear of offending him is rooted in an honest knowledge of ourselves. St Paul reminded himself that he once persecuted the Church. St Augustine knew that he could easily slip back into his former sinful ways. This is honest thinking, and we do well to imitate it. Do not take the risk of driving God away by serious sin. Do not restrain his love by any kind of deliberate sin. In our relationship with him, love and fear work closely together.

It is Never Too Late

St Teresa gives us some signs whereby we can discern the way love and fear work. She is quite eloquent when she speaks of the love of God, and admits she rambles on because she likes to talk about it: 'Those who truly love God, love every good, desire every good, favour every good, praise every good. They always join, favour, and defend good people' (WP 40:3). This love cannot be hidden. It will show itself in language, action, and a consistent way of life. When our love is not so strong, frequent prayer, a sense of our own littleness and a sincere pleading with God to save us from offending him are genuine signs of the beginning of his love in us; and this gives us cause to hope for a greater degree of that love.

No matter how many years have gone by, it is never too late to place ourselves on the way of

God's great gift of love. St Teresa has something special to say about this:

> May it please His Majesty to give us His love before He takes us out of this life, for it will be a great thing at the hour of death to see that we are going to be judged by the One whom we have loved above all things... It will not be like going to a foreign country but like going to our own, because it is the country of one whom we love so much and who loves us. (WP 40:8)

The picture of God that comes through to us in this passage is very revealing. God is the One who loves us and gives us his home to be ours forever. Clearly, his love is to be sought diligently at all times. Those who seek this supreme gift and know their own weakness will try to steer clear of everything that leads them to offend his goodness.

This care not to offend is so strongly advocated by St Teresa that she says we should be willing to die a thousand times, rather than deliberately offend God in a serious way, and that it should be unthinkable for us even in a small matter. Yet she makes it clear that people who get so strict as to be inhuman just turn others away from prayer, and Teresa never intended that:

> strive as much as you can, without offence to God, to be affable and understanding in such a way that everyone you talk to will love your conversation and desire your manner of

living and acting, and not be frightened and intimidated by virtue. (WP 41:7)

So, to sum up Teresa's teaching on this 'inseparable pair': *fear* will make us watch our steps; *love* will quicken our steps – both of them bringing us along the way, on our journey to God.

Appendix
Praying in the Footsteps of St Teresa

St Teresa says prayer is an intimate exchange with him who we know loves us. If we know this, we will find it easier to spend time alone with him – and to do this often.

*

Resolved to Pray

Much has been said and written on prayer, and yet not many people seem to succeed in making prayer a way of life. The difficulty lies, to some extent, in the lack of resolution. This point is so important, so vital, that there is no way to highlight it too much.

Time and again, Teresa appeals to us to make up our minds once and for all: that, come what may, we are going to give time to quiet prayer; and no matter how dull, flat, dry-as-dust it becomes, we will go on and on. Do not think this is too much for you.

The hardest part of praying is to begin. But people who have acquired the habit of giving time regularly to prayer would find it harder to give up than to continue.

St Teresa's idea of God as the one who knows all things, who can do all things and who loves us is worth thinking over at some length.

If God loves you enough to make you out of nothing, and to send to Calvary his beloved Son in whom he was so well pleased, then our tendency to shy away from God is wrong, and lacking in faith and confidence. It takes time and work to reverse this trend, and yet such a change is necessary. Search the Scriptures with the set purpose of learning this lesson from the Holy Spirit.

The King is not put off by our unworthiness. This is what the Incarnation is all about. The song of the angels at Bethlehem gives this message: peace on earth to people who are the object of God's good will. Every book in the Bible should be read in this light.

Awareness of Our Lives

All of the sixteen chapters of the First Letter to the Corinthians are worth careful study in the matter of prayer, to see what is permanent and what is not. But in particular, we can take a few points from the passage quoted and start to work on them day by day. Divide it into some *DOs* and *DON'Ts*. *Don't* be selfish, boastful, resentful. *Do* be kind, patient, forgiving, persevering. Try it – and the concrete situations will emerge. Out of this experiment you will begin to see in yourself some real failures in Christian living. Do not run away from them. The very fact that you can face them will make you a forgiving, tolerant person, slow to condemn and a good, patient listener. This is a solid beginning on which to build.

Each of us can list some of the temptations and evils we want God to keep away from us, be they persons, places or things, and it is good at times to repeat this petition quietly and to mention each of the things we have in mind. This helps to bring our prayer and our day-to-day circumstances together; it makes prayer more real and life more prayerful.

We really need to count our blessings: then we will be able to find the hidden benefits in our trials, to list them clearly, and to thank God for them one by one.

There are many things we have to go without because we cannot afford them. This 'state of being without' is really a place where God is waiting for you. Compare your life with that of Christ. Did he have the thing you regret being unable to afford? Can you find consolation in the fact that you share this lack with him?

We get far too concerned about our health and comfort. St Teresa told her nuns to be 'manly' about such things and not to be preoccupied about small illnesses and unnecessary comforts. Look into the things you do every day, and see: are you over-concerned about health, or perhaps ruining it through lack of discipline? Here again is an area of self-denial, a place to compare yourself with Christ, to deny yourself in ways that will let him live in you.

St Teresa is very strong on 'self-knowledge', and in her language this means something highly practical: we should note objectively how we act or fail to act, ask ourselves why, and try little by little with God's help to change.

In the Likeness of Christ

To learn what God is like, we search the Bible...

Teresa says that when Christ taught us to say, 'Thy will be done', he was asking us to join with him in giving our will to the Father.

We must give our will gladly and make sure that real action follows our promise.

Just as we said about praying to him who we know loves us, so, too, we live our lives each day under the eyes of him who loves us and is pleased with all we do, so long as it is not sinful. This should help us to enjoy doing his will, even when it involves things not pleasant for us. This is the real secret of the saints: to enjoy doing things that are hard for us, in order to please him. Through these, we learn the real wisdom that comes from being close to God. There is no place we can get close to Christ so quickly as in his sufferings.

Teresa says: 'it calls for great humility to be silent at seeing oneself condemned without fault. This is a wonderful way to imitate the Lord who took away all our faults. So, I ask you to take great care about this practice; it brings with it great benefits. I see no reason at all for us to try to excuse ourselves, unless, as I say, in some cases where not telling the truth would cause anger or scandal!'

There are some indications of real humility. Gratitude is one. To be aware of the goodness of God when things are going badly for us – that is humility. To see any good we find in ourselves as a gift of God, to want to be like Christ when he was accused and remained silent – that is his work within us.

Focused on God

It is not enough to give our attention to prayer: we must always be trying to give our life to God.

St Teresa tries to bring a new awareness into our prayer by telling us to ask ourselves three questions before we recite a vocal prayer: To whom am I going to speak? Who am I? What am I going to say?

It is well worth your while to go to the Scriptures to look at people who spoke to God, and see the great awareness they had.

What a senseless thing, to be proud in the face of the fact that we came from nothing and are depending on God every second of our existence.

Even when certain things reassure us of God's presence, we must not cling to them but always focus on God, whom we do not see as long as we live. When faith and trust and humility have grown as evidence of our sincere, generous love, then God lets us know that he is there in the dark. The 'absence' is found to contain the 'presence'.

Lessons in Prayer

To take one method and stay with it, until you have made a habit of it, is a very necessary thing.

When you read a lot about prayer, about schools and methods of prayer and about Eastern ways of deeper awareness, you can fall into the trap of hopping from one method to another. This is fatal because it prevents you from acquiring the perseverance that is so necessary in prayer. Prayer is a part of our life and has its bright days and dull periods for many reasons. No one has ever achieved anything in any field without a lot of patience and real slogging. Many people have given up just when success was within reach, and so a great effort ended in failure. All our good resolutions about perseverance in prayer can be undermined by skipping from one method to another. Those who stay with prayer finally come to a 'way' that is their own personal method; but in the beginning, it is vitally important to select one method and to stay with it. We do not necessarily have to choose St Teresa's method. Her virtue is not in criticising other methods but in following one and showing how it develops.

In one way or another, we need to bend our heart's attention to the fact that God not only calls and invites us to pray, but that Christ prays with us and in us.

Surely, it is no big thing for us to turn away our attention, sometimes, from other attractions and to look at him. 'Well, is it such a big thing that from time to time you turn your eyes to look upon one who gives you so much?'

At the Side of Christ

It is very wise, when you experience trials, to take them to him in his sufferings; and if you can do nothing else, tell him how much you are hurting. Walk the road to Calvary with him.

Take a passage from St Teresa and start to turn it into your own words until you are saying *your* thoughts, making *your* meditations, having *your* conversation with Christ; until *your* pain is joined to his, and you feel his love for you in his sacrifices for you, and you begin to respond and to see that you are not suffering because of your sins or because God does not care, but because he *does* care – because he wants to pull you up into life with himself on a closer level.

Teresa tells us to practise enduring small trials, and to get a picture of Christ and talk to him about them until this becomes a habit. She insists we can do this.

Technique is *not* the big thing; but the will to pray, to get close to him often, until it is a habit, until it is your life – that is the real thing.

Try every way you can to stay at his side. To grow accustomed to this, to make it a solid habit, is what makes a real, unbelievable difference in life. This is the place of opportunity; it is where gold is found, where life begins at any age and goes on eternally.

Right Priorities

This calling God 'our Father' is a matter deserving repeated attention at length. Here is the very centre of your life, the home from which you go out and to which you return. Of its very nature, this relationship with God, your Father, links you to Christ, your Brother, and to all people as your own family.

God gives the strength, the moment we make the effort.

Review our whole set of values until we come more and more to prize the things that last and forget what passes. This change of heart and outlook is an immense help to prayer. It opens the way for God to work in us, and to make us ready for the gifts he has for us.

By saying our vocal prayers well, we can grow in this awareness of God within us, loving us, caring for us – God who made us, God who redeemed us, God who changes us until we are like him.

A Desire for Prayer

Practise this awareness of God often, and do not give up. The habit may be acquired in a year, but we should be willing to work longer. The very effort has its own rewards. All this may be distant from the beginner, but it becomes clearer as we practise recollection. We may have nothing to say, other than the words of prayers we have learnt; but if we say these slowly, they begin to relate to our life and then to Christ's.

The strong desire of the heart to come to Christ is vitally important. A habit of prayer is something to strive for throughout a lifetime. It is God's greatest gift to the soul.

Prayer consecrates us and makes us holy and pleasing to God; it makes us walk the earth with a freer swing, not as slaves of the world but as people who are free in Christ.

Communing with God

When God seems absent and prayer is a kind of blind attention without any kind of detail that we can describe, it is most important we keep it up – just attending to this 'absent' Lord in loving attention that is dark, blind, and devoid of feeling or thoughts that tell us anything.

At Communion time, we are really back to the fountain of life. The answer to all our needs is here. So we call out to God for help and we spell out our needs. But we must bear in mind that he knows a whole lot more about our needs than we do. So there is a lot of wisdom here in just giving our attention to him and letting our wonder and love grow in the strength of his presence – in the light of his love for us.

This is such a still time, full of the dawn. 'Be with Him willingly; don't lose so good an occasion for conversing with Him as is the hour after having received Communion.'

We begin to pray by placing ourselves before God. In every way we can, we should return to this most important basic position – the reality of being face to face with God.

Depending on God

The strength we experience on a certain day may be gone the next day; and the assurance which carries us through a whole decade may desert us and leave us without the courage to tackle any situation. St Teresa said this happened to her so regularly that she came to see that whatever virtue she had was just on loan; she is particularly anxious that we take heed of that lesson.

We work from a basis of being redeemed sinners. So we come to the work of pleasing our loving Father with the knowledge that we have within us the ability, and even the inclination, to offend him; indeed, we have a history and habit of offending him.

God has to keep us humble, because this reflects what we are. If we hold onto this truth, he can give us the virtue we need when we need it. If we make the mistake of thinking that the courage or detachment God has given us is something we have acquired and now own, he must leave us without this ability so that we come back to the truth about ourselves.

God gives each new day, and we use it all in his service. The next day we ask again for everything we need to serve him, and for that alone.

With Trials and Worries

When God sends us trials, it is most important that we notice the good they do us and thank him for that. Not so easy but very Christ-like.

It is a very good thing to talk to God and tell him just what worries us and why. If we keep doing this, we are bound to begin to see that he controls all the things about which we worry.

We are anxious because we are not in control – we must learn to be happy that *he* is in control. This is a difficult lesson to learn, and yet we cannot afford to live without it.

St Teresa gives a very valuable piece of advice, and all who feel they do not belong close to God should take it to heart and put it into practice regularly: 'When you find yourselves in this condition, stop thinking about your misery, insofar as possible, and turn your thoughts to the mercy of God, to how He loves us and suffered for us.'

Journeying in Hope

Teresa says that people who say the Our Father sincerely will not go astray.

'Prayer is a safe road; you will be more quickly freed from temptation when close to the Lord than when far.' And that surely makes a whole lot of sense.

To Teresa, 'Deliver us from evil' was a request to be brought immediately into the everlasting joys of heaven. Her own eloquent outburst may be beyond our own reactions, but it is worth our while to reflect that we must pass on from here and that no one has seen, heard or even imagined the good things awaiting us. This exercise of joyful hope is a great way to become detached from all the things we cling to with a mere finger-hold.

Ultimately, we are asking that, in the end, heaven will be ours and we will be saved from all evil. It is the big request that we should make with confidence. We are talking to God who can give us anything and wants with all his heart to give us everything.

*

Prayer is the gift of God to anyone who believes in his love and speaks to him humbly, sincerely, frequently, and with the faithful perseverance that love requires. It is possible for you and me.

Sources Quoted

Quotations from the prose works of St Teresa are taken from the following edition:

The Collected Works of St. Teresa of Avila, 3 vols., trs. Kieran Kavanaugh, OCD & Otilio Rodriguez, OCD, Washington, DC: ICS Publications, 1987, 1980 & 1985.

The Way of Perfection can be found in Volume 2.

There are two versions of St Teresa's *Way of Perfection*, both believed to have been written in around 1566: the Escorial and Valladolid manuscripts, named after the places where they are kept; see note 1 for further details. Modern editions generally follow the Valladolid (later) version, incorporating certain passages from the Escorial manuscript in brackets, italics, or in notes. Those Escorial passages which are not included in the ICS edition, and which are quoted in this book, are taken from the translation of E Allison Peers: see notes 5-9 for full details of these particular passages.

Notes

1. The two versions (both written in around 1566) are named after the places where the manuscripts are kept: the first version being known as the 'Escorial' manuscript (kept in the royal library of 'El Escorial', the royal palace outside Madrid), the second one as the 'Valladolid' manuscript (which can be found in the Carmelite monastery in that city). References to Escorial passages will appear in later notes, where relevant (as explained in 'Sources Quoted'). The Valladolid version, previously considered to date from 1569, is now believed to have been written probably at the end of 1566 or the beginning of 1567: see Tomás Alvarez, OCD, *St. Teresa of Avila: 100 Themes on Her Life and Work*, Washington, DC: ICS Publications, 2011, p. 314.

2. Vatican II, *Lumen Gentium* (*Dogmatic Constitution on the Church*), # 5; italics have been added here.

3. These words were written by the Columban Missionary Fr John Henaghan, in his *Pathways to God*, Dublin: Carmelite Centre of Spirituality / Bury, Greater Manchester: Koinonia ('Living Flame Series', vol. 13), 1981, p. 7.

4. Vatican II, *Dei Verbum* (*Dogmatic Constitution*

on Divine Revelation), # 2; paragraph 1 of this document is a very short Preface, so the passage quoted here is, in effect, the opening of *Dei Verbum*.

5. A passage from the Escorial manuscript of *The Way of Perfection*, in *The Complete Works of Saint Teresa of Jesus*, vol. II, tr. & ed. E Allison Peers, London: Sheed & Ward, 1946, p. 157. (A facsimile of this translation is currently available, published by Burns & Oates in 2002.)

6. *Ibid.*, pp. 161-2. The first of the three sentences in this quotation comes from the Escorial manuscript; it is given the paragraph numbering here of WP 37:3, but technically it occurs between the end of WP 37:2 and the beginning of WP 37:3 in the Valladolid version.

7. *Ibid.*, p. 165 – a phrase from the Escorial manuscript.

8. *Ibid.*, p. 168; this sentence from the Escorial manuscript occurs in a passage after WP 38:9 and is given that reference here, as it is the final paragraph number in Chapter 38 of the Valladolid version.

9. *Ibid.*, p. 185; the second sentence of this quotation comes from the Escorial manuscript.

TERESIAN PRESS
PUBLICATIONS AVAILABLE

The Writings of St Teresa of Avila: An Introduction
Eugene McCaffrey, OCD
£5.00

John of the Cross: Seasons of Prayer
Iain Matthew, OCD
£5.00

Infinite Horizons: Scripture through Carmelite Eyes
James McCaffrey, OCD
£8.00

Elizabeth of the Trinity: The Unfolding of her Message
Joanne Mosley
2 volumes, £10.00 each volume

Holiness For All: Themes from St Thérèse of Lisieux
Aloysius Rego, OCD
£7.00

Upon This Mountain: Prayer in the Carmelite Tradition
Mary McCormack, OCD
£4.00

Let Yourself Be Loved: Elizabeth of the Trinity
Eugene McCaffrey, OCD
£5.00

Teresian Press
Carmelite Priory
Boars Hill
Oxford OX1 5HB

www.carmelitebooks.com

TERESIAN PRESS
SOME FORTHCOMING PUBLICATIONS

Living with God: St Teresa's Understanding of Prayer
Tomás Álvarez, OCD

A Moment of Prayer – A Life of Prayer
Conrad De Meester, OCD

The Our Father: St Teresa of Avila's Catechism of Prayer
Aloysius Rego, OCD

*Captive Flames: A Biblical Reading of
the Carmelite Saints – **to be reissued***
James McCaffrey, OCD

*Journey of Love: Teresa of Avila's Interior Castle
– A Reader's Guide*
Eugene McCaffrey, OCD

What Carmel Means to Me
Edited by James McCaffrey, OCD & Joanne Mosley

Teresian Press
Carmelite Priory
Boars Hill
Oxford OX1 5HB

www.carmelitebooks.com